The Word (

God's Three Short Letters To Believers Through John

Roger Henri Trepanier

© 2017

This book is dedicated to all those on earth who believe what God said through His servant John at 1 John 4:15,

"Whoever confesses that Jesus is the Son of God, God abides in him, and he in God."

Titles available from Roger Henri Trepanier in
The Truth Seeker's Library™ series:

God Did Not Create Human Beings To Die… But To Live On…
Eternally!
Finding Comfort And Encouragement In The Promises Of God In The
Last Days
How We Know For Sure That We Are Living In The Last Days!
Have You Ever Wondered What Happens After Death?
An Introduction To The New World That Is Coming On The Earth
Deeper Truths Of The Christian Life
Evangelism As God Intended
Keeping On Serving God In The Last Days
The Mysterious World Of Angels And Demons
No One Loves As He Loves!
Thanks Be To God For His Indescribable Gift!
The Church Is Very Much Alive, Well, And Growing!
Tracing The Steps Of The Son Of God From Eternity To Eternity!
War, And Going To War, Is Simply Not Of God!
God Never Meant Prayer To Be A Mystery!
Health Is One Of God's Great Blessings!
Removing The Mystery Surrounding Baptism!
This World's Return To Paganism Is Almost Complete!

Titles available from Roger Henri Trepanier in
The Practical Helps Library™ series:

Learning to Overcome The Perplexities Of This Present Life
So, I Hear You Want To Work With Seniors?
I Will Not Have This Man To Rule Over Me!
Spiritual Truth To Warm The Heart!
Fasten Your Seatbelts: Turbulence Ahead!
Living A Normal Christian Life In An Increasingly Abnormal World!

Titles available from Roger Henri Trepanier
in The Christian Fiction Library™ series:

The Beginning Of A New Dawn
It Is Never Too Late For Love!
The True To Life Musings Of Fred And Ernie
Between A Rock And A Hard Place!
Love Knows No Boundaries!

A Woman Worth Pursuing!
Love Is More Than Just A Four Letter Word!

**Other Titles available from Roger Henri Trepanier
in The Word Of God Library™ series:**

God's First Letter To The Thessalonians
God's Second Letter To The Thessalonians
God's Letter To Believers Through Jude

INTRODUCTION

This is the fourth book in the series titled, "The Word of God Library." God is leading His servant to have a few commentaries published of various books of God's word, the Bible, that have been written over the years. While these commentaries are expository in nature (that is, explained in some detail), they are still intended to be devotional, heartwarming, and as practical as possible, to help believers live out their faith in these last days of the present age. There are also three sections to the Addendum dealing with: 1) the four ages of time; 2) the two separate comings from Heaven to earth in time of God's Son, The Lord Jesus Christ; and 3) how one may have a personal relationship with God, if there are any readers who do not already have this vital relationship. It is highly recommended that one start with the Addendum before one begins to read the book.

This particular book deals with the three short letters that God had the apostle John write down for us, which are called First John, Second John, and Third John. In each one of these letters God addresses a specific subject that He wanted us as believers yet on earth to be aware of during our time here. Apart from these three short letters, God also had the apostle John write down 'The Gospel According To John' and also the book known as 'The Revelation.'

What should also be mentioned before closing this Introduction is that after completing 21 years of formal education and then spending almost 28 years working in Project Engineering and Management in the Corporate offices of a large utility, God called His servant as a non-denominational evangelist in early 1999, and then sent him out a few thousand miles, away from family and friends, to the place of service God assigned, which is where His servant has been and is still serving Him as evangelist, counselor, author, editor, and publisher. The author is a widower with three adopted children, all now married with a family of their own.

Please note the two websites listed below, which have been established for the purpose of interacting with readers and for gospel ministry:

http://www.pilgrimpathwaypublications.com

http://servantofmosthigh.com

And now my prayer is that God will richly bless you as you read this book, and greatly minister to your every need in your life as only God can! To Him be all praise, honor, and glory, with thanksgiving, forevermore! Amen.

CONTENTS

SECTION 1

First John

CHAPTER ONE

1 John 1:1-10

A brief introduction

Unlike most of the other letters of the New Testament, where God identifies the believer through whom He is giving His word (for instance, the letters written down by Paul, Peter, James, and Jude), yet in these three short letters known as First John, Second John, and Third John, God does not identify the writer. However, we do know that it was the apostle John whom God chose to write down His word for us as believers in these three short letters simply from the internal evidence in the letters themselves, as we will see. The apostle John was one of the twelve apostles of God's Son, The Lord Jesus Christ, who walked with Him daily during the three and half years of His public ministry, having also been chosen of God write down two major books of the New Testament, that being "The Gospel According To John," and "The Revelation." What is interesting to further note is that while John is also not referred to by name in his gospel account, yet he is in book of Revelation.

God had the apostle John write First John in order that believers coming after him might also enjoy the fellowship with God through His Son that he himself enjoyed while on earth

Just imagine being chosen of God to walk daily on earth for three and half years with God's own Son, The Lord Jesus Christ, now come from Heaven to be in human flesh, as was the case with the apostle John. This is something that one can never forget and must have been a thrilling experience. And so, God has the apostle John begin this letter by speaking about his own personal experience of walking for three and half years with the most important Person that one can ever encounter and speak about, which is God's own precious Son, The Lord Jesus Christ!

And so, we note from 1 John 1:1-4, that God leads John to write, "**[1] What was from the beginning, what we have heard, what we have seen with our eyes, what we have looked at and touched with our hands, concerning the Word of Life — [2] and the life was manifested, and we have seen and testify and proclaim to you the eternal life, which was with the Father and was manifested to us — [3] what we have seen and heard we proclaim to you also, so that you too may have fellowship with us; and indeed our fellowship is with the Father, and with His Son Jesus Christ. [4] These things we write, so that our joy may be made complete.**"

It is clear from what we read here that this is a first person account of one who has had the life-changing experience of walking with God's Son, The Lord Jesus Christ, while He was here on earth at His first coming from Heaven to earth, "what we have heard…seen with our eyes… looked at and touched with our hands." John would have heard, seen, and looked at God's Son when He was first called of Him to follow Him, as we see at Matthew 4:21,22. And he would have touched our Lord Jesus Christ when he was allowed to rest on His bosom, as we see at John 13:23-25.

When John says here, "What was from the beginning (Greek "Arche")… concerning the Word of Life," he is not referring to the beginning of when God's Son first started His public ministry on earth (which went for three and half years, from 29 to 33 AD, ending when He died at the cross), but rather God is here referring to the same "beginning" as is in view at John 1:1,2, where God there says, adding verse 3 and 14 for context, "[1] In the beginning ("Arche") was the Word (The Son, verse 14), and the Word was with God (The Father), and the Word was God (that is, they were of the same essence, noting Hebrews 1:2,3; Colossians 1:15-17). [2] He (The Son) was in the beginning ("Arche") with God (The Father)…[3] All things came into being through Him (The Son), and apart from Him nothing came into being that has come into being… [14] And the (eternally existing Son as the) Word became flesh, and dwelt among us, and we saw

His glory, glory as of the only begotten from the Father, full of grace and truth."

As we see from verse 14 here, the "Word" is a title for God's Son, which He has had from the beginning, with that "beginning" being when "all things came into being," as we see at verse 3, which is when this original creation that we are now part of first occurred, which is when time also started to be marked. God gives us an account of this at Genesis 1 in the Old Testament. And what is critical to grasp here is that God's Son did not acquire the title of "the Word" only at the time of creation, but rather has always had that title as the eternally existing Son of God.

But what did take place for the first time, which was at creation, is when God The Father spoke all that has been created into existence from nothing (Hebrews 11:3), which was done through His Son, as The Word! So when God says at John 1:3, "All things came into being through Him (The Son)," it is the same as what we read at Genesis 1:3 at the beginning of creation, "Then God said, "Let there be light"; and there was light." " In other words, God was there bringing into existence the "light," as all that was to be brought into existence through His Son, The Word.

Then when God has John, at 1 John 1:1, refer to God's Son, now in human flesh, as "the Word of Life," we are to see that here He is making reference to Him as we see at John 1:4, where God stated regarding His precious Son, The Lord Jesus Christ, "In Him was life, and the life was the Light of men." So the term "Word of Life" is yet another title for God's Son, now in human flesh, since in Him was the life of God, which is eternal life, since God's Son is eternal. That is why God refers to that life as being eternal life at 1 John 1:2, where God says, "and the life was manifested, and we have seen and testify and proclaim to you the eternal life, which was with the Father and was manifested to us (through God's Son now coming to earth" in human flesh). That is also why God's Son could say while on earth what has been recorded for us at John 14:6, "Jesus said to him, "I am the way, and the truth, and the LIFE; no one comes to the Father but through Me." "

And that life is "the Light of men" simply because those who now receive that eternal life with God through faith in His Son at salvation are no longer in the darkness of sin, as all unbelievers on earth are, but are now "sons of Light," as we see God refer to such at John 12:36a, "While you have the Light, believe in the Light, so that you may become sons of Light." That is also why God's Son told His followers while on earth at His first coming what we read at John 8:12, "Then Jesus again spoke to them, saying, "I am the Light of the world; he who follows Me will not walk in the darkness, but will have the Light of life." " And those who have the life of God through salvation no longer walk in darkness, since they now have the light of God's word as illuminated by The Holy Spirit to guide them spiritually on the path of life here on earth daily, as we read at Psalm 119:105, "Your word is a lamp to my feet and a light to my path."

Then at 1 John 1:3, God discloses the reason for why He has given this first letter to us through the apostle John, "what we have seen and heard we proclaim to you also, so that you too may have fellowship with us; and indeed our fellowship is with the Father, and with His Son Jesus Christ." And so we see that God had the apostle John write this first letter in order that believers coming after him might also enjoy the fellowship with God through His Son, The Lord Jesus Christ, that the apostle John himself enjoyed while he was on earth in literally walking daily with God's own precious Son.

What we need to realize here as believers, and ever keep in mind, is that none of us is ever saved by God in any age of time just for our own sake, but rather God chooses us as His own in salvation (2 Thessalonians 2:13,14) in order that we might not only be His witnesses while here on earth, but that we might also serve Him while we are here! In other words, let us never forget that we have been saved in order to serve, that is, to do God's will, which is never a burden, but always a delight. Let us never allow the devil to rob us of the blessing that comes in serving God by carrying out His will while on earth. Many times I catch myself saying to God, "I will pass through this life only once, which is only a very short time in the light of eternity, therefore, may my time here be for Your glory, honor, and praise!' So that is why John is led of God to conclude at 1 John 1:4, "These things we write, so that our joy may be made complete."

As we grow in the knowledge of God through His word and as we mature in the faith as God's children after salvation, we come to realize that we are one body spiritually with every other believer on earth, with one Head in Heaven, that being God's own Son, The Lord

Jesus Christ! Let us note what God discloses to us in this regard at 1 Corinthians 12:12,13,27, "[12] For even as the (physical) body is one and yet has many members, and all the members of the (physical) body, though they are many, are one body, so also is Christ. [13] For by one (Holy) Spirit we were all baptized (spiritually, as a work of God by His Spirit) into one body (at the moment of our salvation), whether Jews or Greeks, whether slaves or free, and we were all made to drink of one Spirit... [27] Now you are Christ's (spiritual) body, and individually members of it." That is why the apostle John is led of God to say here at 1 John 1:4 that his joy is made complete when we too as believers experience spiritual fellowship with God The Father through His Son, The Lord Jesus Christ, by The Holy Spirit now indwelling in our human spirit; simply because John is aware not only of all believers on earth being one spiritually with God The Father through His Son by The Spirit, but also why His Son was manifested in human flesh on earth, that we might come to have fellowship with God and His Son after having believed in Him!

John is then led of God to disclose how believers can maintain their spiritual fellowship with God moment by moment

Let us always remember that our spiritual fellowship with God The Father is through His Son, The Lord Jesus Christ, by The Holy Spirit, simply because our access to God The Father is always through His Son by The Spirit! That is why our prayers are always to God The Father in Jesus' Name, by the enablement of The Holy Spirit (John 16:23,26). And so now here at 1 John 1, John is led of God to continue and disclose to believers how one can maintain one's spiritual fellowship with God The Father through His Son by The Spirit, which we all enter at the moment of our salvation, with John also disclosing here how we can lose that fellowship, noting what we now read at 1 John 1:5-7, "[5] **This is the message we have heard from Him and announce to you, that God is Light, and in Him there is no darkness at all. [6] If we say that we have fellowship with Him and yet walk in the darkness, we lie and do not practice the truth; [7] but if we walk in the Light as He Himself is in the Light, we have fellowship with one another, and the blood of Jesus His Son cleanses us from all sin.**"

When we read here at 1 John 1:5, "God is Light, and in Him there is no darkness at all," we need to realize that God is speaking of the fact that He is absolutely pure, holy, eternally untainted by sin! What this means then is that the "Light" here speaks of the absence of sin, while the "darkness" speaks of the presence of sin! Therefore, the only way that believers can ever maintain their fellowship with God after salvation is to constantly remain free from known unconfessed sins in one's life! That is why God says what He does at 1 John 1:6 here, "If we say that we have fellowship with Him and yet walk in darkness (that is, with known unconfessed sins in our lives), we lie and do not practice the truth." God sees all at all times, and so He knows when we have known unconfessed sins in our lives or not. We might be able to fool other human beings, who cannot see the condition of our hearts; but we can never fool God, Who always knows the condition of our hearts (1 Samuel 16:7; Hebrews 4:13)!

And so after telling us how known unconfessed sins prevents us from spiritual fellowship with God, God then goes on and discloses how we can maintain continual fellowship with Him, as His children after salvation, as we see at 1 John 1:7, "but if we walk in the Light as He Himself is in the Light, we have fellowship with one another, and the blood of Jesus His Son cleanses us from all sin." As we have seen, to walk in the Light is to walk with no unconfessed sins in our lives, which means that when we so walk, with no known unconfessed sins in our lives, then we have continual fellowship with God The Father through His Son, The Lord Jesus Christ, by The Holy Spirit, since God The Father is always "in the Light," being always free from sin. What God is trying to make us realize here is that known unconfessed sins in our lives breaks our spiritual fellowship with Him, noting what He tells us at Isaiah 59:2, "But your iniquities have made a separation between you and your God, and your sins have hidden His face from you so that He does not hear." Now we are to live in the light since God is Light and in Him there is no darkness at all.

What we are to realize here, based on what God says at 1 John 1:7, is that when we walk with no known unconfessed sins in our lives, we not only have fellowship with God The Father and The Son of God, but we also have spiritual fellowship with other believers, who are so walking with God! Unbelievers may sometimes meet someone and realize that they have come in contact with 'a kindred soul.' However, we as believers, when we come across another believer walking with God, we say that we have come in contact with 'a kindred spirit!'

What is also true of all believers who walk with God with no known unconfessed sins in one's life is that "the blood of Jesus His Son cleanses us from all sin." What this means is that God sees us in the same spiritual condition we were in at the moment of our salvation. When we first believed in God through believing the gospel concerning His Son (Romans 1:1,3; 1 Corinthians 15:1-4), we had all our sins forgiven, based on God's Son, The Lord Jesus Christ, having spilt His lifeblood at the cross, when He died to pay the penalty of death due our sins. And so, when we continue to walk with God subsequent to salvation with no known unconfessed sins in our lives, then "the blood of Jesus" continues to be applied to our lives by God, so that we can walk with God in the Light moment by moment!

God goes on to disclose what is the ONLY remedy for known unconfessed sins in the lives of believers

What is now very important to note is that God has made a provision for believers to be forgiven any sins committed subsequent to salvation, for believers still unfortunately have a sinful nature that wants us to live in opposition to how God wants us to live, which means that whenever we do give in to our sinful nature, we sin against God, simply because now we are no longer walking in the Light as He is in the Light! So God knows this is our situation, so He has made provision for us to go on walking with Him after salvation, which He now discloses in the truths He shares with us at 1 John 1:8-10, where we read, "[8] **If we say that we have no sin, we are deceiving ourselves and the truth is not in us. [9] If we confess our sins, He is faithful and righteous to forgive us our sins and to cleanse us from all unrighteousness. [10] If we say that we have not sinned, we make Him a liar and His word is not in us**."

And so as to not go astray here, we need to realize at the outset that when God speaks of "sin" here at verse 8, He is speaking of our sinful nature in us, and is not speaking about a specific act of sin, such as lying or stealing. That sinful nature is what all human beings have since the time Adam and Eve - our first parents from whom the whole of the human race is derived from in time - sinned against God and incurred that sinful nature. That sinful nature is passed on through the male at procreation, which is why when God's Son came from Heaven to earth, He was born of a virgin, so as to not incur that sinful nature; instead taking on the sinless body prepared for Him by

19

His Father (Hebrews 10:5). And so all human beings have this sinful nature at birth, which does not become active until the age of accountability, which is the age at which a child learns right from wrong and chooses the wrong, thereby sinning against God, since acting from one's sinful nature. From that moment on, the child is accountable to God for one's own sin against Him, having become a sinner. This is what God wants believers to acknowledge and not deny at 1 John 1:8, the fact that we all have a sinful nature.

Then at 1 John 1:9, God goes on to give the ONLY remedy that He ever provides for when a believer sins AFTER salvation, after having been cleansed of all sins committed against God from the age of accountability onwards, and that remedy is to confess all known unconfessed sins to God, as He tells us to here, "If we confess our sins, He is faithful and righteous to forgive us our sins and to cleanse us from all unrighteousness." And let us not go astray into false teaching of any kind here, for we are instructed by God to confess our known unconfessed sins committed after salvation TO HIM. That it is to God that we confess our sins, and not to some human being, is clear from what God goes on to say here, when He says, "HE is faithful and righteous to forgive us..." Confession brings immediate forgiveness and complete cleansing from all unrighteousness committed, which is always against Him, for all sin is always against God, noting what we read at Psalm 51:4, "Against You, You only, I have sinned and done what is evil in Your sight, so that You are justified when You speak and blameless when You judge."

And let us never forget that the basis that God uses to forgive our sins after salvation is the same as the basis He uses to forgive our sins the first time at the moment of first believing in Him through His Son at salvation, which is the death of God's Son at the cross, where The Son of God, The Lord Jesus Christ, already died to pay the penalty for those sins ever committed against God in time by all human beings. This is something God makes very clear at 1 Peter 2:24 in part, "and He Himself bore our sins in His body on the cross, so that we might die to sin and live to righteousness..." God's intent for His own after salvation is that we no longer live as we did before salvation, which was always living out of our sinful nature, and so always sinning against Him, since all thoughts, actions, and words coming from our sinful nature are all acts of sin against God. Rather, after salvation God would have us live by His righteousness, which is

20

His own imparted life, which He imparts to us through His Son by His Spirit in us.

We are further told by God at 1 Peter 3:18 in part, "For Christ also died for sins once for all, the just for the unjust, so that He might bring us to God..." As we read here, it was "once and for all" that God's Son "died for sins," He Who had no sin, dying in the place of the sinner. And now that we have life with God through faith in His Son, we are to go on living by that life after salvation, which is God's righteousness, which He automatically imparts to us by His Holy Spirit in us when we walk with no known unconfessed sins in our lives. That is why God says at the end of 1 John 1:9 that confession of known unconfessed sins from us brings forgiveness of those sins from Him, and also cleansing "from all unrighteousness," because living by our sinful nature is living by our own life, or righteousness, which God here calls "unrighteousness;" instead of living by God's life, or righteousness. And that is also why God says at the end of 1 Peter 2:24, "that we might die to sin and live to righteousness," since His desire for His own is always that we die to our sinful nature, so as to live by His imparted life, moment by moment after salvation, which is His imparted life, or righteousness!

Then at 1 John 1:10, God addresses another potential problem that a believer might encounter after salvation, which is to want to deny acts of sin in one's life, as God says here, "If we say that we have not sinned, we make Him a liar and His word is not in us." What God is addressing here is the fact that since He indwells us by His Spirit, He is very much aware of any sins that we might commit. And the moment that sin occurs, He lets us know in an unmistakable fashion, by convicting us regarding that sin by removing His peace and His joy, including the suspension of His imparted life, which we enjoy with Him when we walk with Him with no known unconfessed sins in our lives.

We would greatly benefit noting one very specific example of the application of 1 John 1:9 and 10 in the life of a believer, which was king David of old, noting what God tells us at Psalm 32:3-5, "[3] When I kept silent about my sin, my body wasted away through my groaning all day long. [4] For day and night Your hand was heavy upon me; my vitality was drained away as with the fever heat of summer. Selah. [5] I acknowledged my sin to You, and my iniquity I did not hide; I said, "I will confess my transgressions to the Lord"; and You forgave the guilt of my sin. Selah."

And before closing the first chapter of First John, we need to be aware of another potential problem here, which God does not mention at this point, but which is nevertheless very real in the life of a believer, usually a new one in particular, and that is to think that we are no longer a Christian because we have sinned against God, especially if we regard it as a grievous sin. The devil is the one we served, usually unknowingly, before we came to personally know God at salvation; and after we come to know God and start serving Him, then the devil becomes our enemy and he will from that day onwards do everything in his power to attempt to stop us from walking with God, one way being to get us to sin. And when we do, then he tries to convince us that now we have lost our salvation, and accuses us over and over again. Even while this is going on, God has not abandoned us, of course. But at the same time, He wants us to realize that there is a consequence to sin as a child of His. The devil always makes sin look enticing, but it always leaves us dejected and feeling guilty afterwards. This is as God intends, for then we will come to hate sinning against God and desire more and more to walk with Him by His own imparted righteousness, which we will do as we continue with Him with no known unconfessed sins in our lives!

So it is very important to know that we cannot lose our salvation! The saying, 'Once saved, always saved,' is true! And there are two reasons at least why this is so. The first is that our salvation is wholly a work of God's grace and power alone, and He can never fail in what He does. In fact, salvation is a gift that we did not deserve, but which God nevertheless graciously bestowed upon us. Here is what He says at Ephesians 2:8-10, "[8] For by grace (God's unmerited favor) you have been saved through faith (believing); and that not of yourselves, it is the gift of God; [9] not as a result of works, so that no one may boast. [10] For we are His workmanship, created in Christ Jesus (speaking of the moment of our salvation) for good works, which God prepared beforehand so that we would walk in them." And so, since salvation is a work which God does, and He can never fail, then that means that we cannot lose that salvation once He gives it to us as a free gift.

Then secondly, we cannot lose our salvation simply because God likens that salvation to a spiritual birth into His family, which it is, very much like when we entered this world through a physical birth. So just like we cannot undo a physical birth into our earthly family, no matter how badly we might behave in that family – and we all do - then similarly we cannot undo a spiritual birth into God's family at salvation, when He forgives us all our past sins and gives us eternal life through His Son by His Holy Spirit, at the moment we come to believe the gospel concerning His Son, The Lord Jesus Christ!

Let us note here also what God says in His word first in regards to this being a work of God, noting John 1:12,13, "[12] But as many as received Him, to them He gave the right to become children of God, even to those who believe in His name, [13] WHO WERE BORN, not of blood nor of the will of the flesh nor of the will of man, but OF GOD," and then secondly in regards to our salvation being likened to a physical birth, noting here John 3:5-7, "[5] Jesus answered, "Truly, truly, I say to you, unless one is born of water and the Spirit he cannot enter into the kingdom of God. [6] That which is born of the flesh is flesh (speaking of a physical birth), and that which is born of the Spirit is spirit (speaking of a spiritual birth). [7] Do not be amazed that I said to you, 'You must be born again.' " In other words, just as one experiences a physical birth to enter this world, so too one must experience a spiritual birth to enter the Kingdom of God, which is Heaven.

CHAPTER TWO

1 John 2:1-29

As we begin the second chapter of First John, we need to realize that the chapter and verse divisions were included by human beings after God's word had been given to us (Chapter divisions 1227 AD; verse divisions, 1551 AD for New Testament and 1571 AD for Old Testament). In other words, the chapter and verse divisions are not of God. This is being mentioned here simply because the first two verses of the second chapter of First John deal with the subject of sin that we have just been looking at when we looked at 1 John 1:8-10 in the first chapter. That is to say, it would have been better to have included 1 John 2:1,2 as part of chapter one, rather than chapter two, as we will now see in examining these two first verses of chapter two, "[1] **My little children, I am writing these things to you so that you may not sin. And if anyone sins, we have an Advocate with the Father, Jesus Christ the righteous; [2] and He Himself is the propitiation for our sins; and not for ours only, but also for those of the whole world.**"

In God saying in the first verse here, "My little children," He is addressing those who are His children by spiritual birth into His family from the moment of salvation onwards. And when God adds through the apostle John, "I am writing these things to you so that you may not sin," He is now making reference to the subject of sin, which He has been dealing with since introducing the subject at 1 John 1:8-10. And that is why it was stated above that these two verses should have been included at the end of 1 John chapter one. Nevertheless, even if added here, we are to see that it is not God's desire that any of His children sin, same as it is not the desire of any parents on earth to see their children sin either. Just as parents on earth know that their children are going astray when their children sin, so too does God know that His children here on earth are also going astray when they sin. It is even more painful for God to see His children sin, since as we have seen sin is always against Him, since we are siding with the devil in opposition to God whenever we sin by acting out of our sinful nature.

However, God being God, He knows that as long as we have a sinful nature, we will sin, and there is a very important reason for saying that here. That is to say, there is a very, very important truth which must be brought out at this point, and it is this: That unless God upholds us in our walk with Him, we automatically act out of our sinful nature and sin against Him. In other words, our sinful nature is our natural nature that will automatically exert itself unless God intervenes to supernaturally enable us to walk with Him! Think of it as His Hand undergirding us moment by moment; so that as long as His Hand is there upholding us, we are walking with Him in the Light as He is in the Light. However, if He removes His Hand for even a moment, we automatically act out of our sinful nature.

What this means then is that when God reveals that our salvation is from Him, He does not only mean having our sins forgiven and our reception of eternal life at the moment of first coming to personally know Him; but rather He wants us to understand that ALL of our life subsequent to salvation is wholly a work of God's grace and power! And at this point, we would do well to speak of God's grace again, which was introduced in the first chapter at Ephesians 2:8, where we saw that salvation is a work of God's grace. Now we are to further see that this salvation includes our daily walk with God after salvation! Let us note what the apostle Paul was led of God to write at 1 Corinthians 15:10 regarding his life and ministry after the moment of his salvation, "But by the GRACE of God I am what I am, and His GRACE toward me did not prove vain; but I labored even more than all of them, yet not I, but the GRACE of God with me."

In other words, all that the apostle Paul was enabled to accomplish after His salvation was wholly a work of God's grace! It was God in him doing His work through His Holy Spirit in him, noting what God says at Philippians 2:13, which is true of all believers, "for it is God who is at work in you, both to will and to work for His good pleasure." That is to say, God indwells a believer by The Holy Spirit from the moment of one's salvation onward for the purpose of carrying on His work on earth through that believer, same as He did through His own Son while He was on earth at His first coming! That is why God tells his children yet on earth what He does at 1 Corinthians 1:30,31, "[30] But by His doing you are in Christ Jesus, who became to us wisdom from God, and righteousness and sanctification, and redemption, [31] so that, just as it is written, "Let him who boasts, boast in the Lord." " Since God is the author of not only our initial salvation (Hebrews 12:1), but also of the whole of our lives afterward, then it is only right that He receive all the praise and the glory for the outworking of our lives!

Coming back now to 1 John 2:1, we note that God then continues, after saying that it was His desire that those who are His own not sin, by now adding, "And if anyone sins, we have an Advocate with the Father, Jesus Christ the righteous…" And in God saying here to His own children, that is, believers yet on earth, "And if anyone sins…," it is obvious that He knows full well that we still have a sinful nature and will sin whenever we are left on our own without His Divine intervention, as was mentioned above. Therefore, that is why God adds what He does here, letting us know what His precious Son is doing in Heaven at His right Hand since He ascended there almost 2000 years ago (Acts 1:9-11), which is to be an Advocate before Him on our behalf whenever we do sin against God. The word "Advocate" here is "Parakletos" in the Greek by which these letters came to us as originally given by God, which word means one who comes to one's aid in terms of interceding on one's behalf.

What is important to realize and keep in mind here is that God's precious Son, "Jesus Christ the righteous," has not only the right to be our Advocate before God The Father in Heaven on behalf of sinners, but He is in Himself the basis for God The Father forgiving the sins of His children on earth when they come to Him confessing their sins, as we further see from 1 John 2:2 here, "and He Himself is the propitiation for our sins; and not for ours only, but also for those of the whole world." The word "propitiation" here is "Hilasmos" in the original, and speaks of the fact that God's Son is in Himself the sacrifice offered to God The Father in His death at the cross as payment for sins; not only, as we further see here, for the sins of believers, but also in payment for the sins of the whole world, even of those who do not believe in God. Two verses which we need to notice here are what God tells us at 2 Corinthians 5:14,15, "[14] For the love of Christ controls us, having concluded this, that one died for all, therefore all died; [15] and He died for all, so that they who live (believers, from the moment of salvation onwards) might no longer live for themselves, but for Him who died and rose again on their behalf."

Therefore, how encouraging it is for believers to know that God's Son, The Lord Jesus Christ, is not only the basis by which God forgives our sins when we confess them to Him, but even when we sin after salvation, He is still helping us by interceding on our behalf before His Father! This is love that is hard for us to comprehend, since it is unconditional, in that it is freely given without our having ever earned it. No wonder we read later at 1 John 3:16 in part, "We know love by this, that He laid down His life for us...," and also at Romans 5:6, "For while we were still helpless, at the right time Christ died for the ungodly."

But before going on here, there is something else that we need to notice, which is that God The Father refers to His Son as "Jesus Christ the righteous," relating to His being our Advocate before The Father's throne in Heaven. One passage which would be helpful in noting at this point in order to understand why He referred to His Son in this way is Hebrews 4:14-16, "[14] Therefore, since we have a great high priest who has passed through the heavens, Jesus the Son of God, let us hold fast our confession. [15] For we do not have a high priest who cannot sympathize with our weaknesses, but One who has been tempted in all things as we are, yet without sin. [16] Therefore let us draw near with confidence to the throne of grace, so that we may receive mercy and find grace to help in time of need."

What needs to be noticed about this passage is that it was given by God to help believers at a time when one has sinned against God. And so, God begins here by reminding believers that we need to hold fast our confession at such times as when we have sinned against God and have come to confess it to Him, since we have a great High Priest, God's own Son, Who is now at His right Hand, but when on earth as a Man, He too was tempted in all things as we are, yet He was ever without sin, being The Son of God. What this means then is that He can sympathize in what we are going through here on earth, in terms of the temptations that we face daily. So that is why God encourages believers at verse 16 to come to His throne of grace with confidence, where we will receive mercy from Him and His grace in order that we might carry on serving Him here on earth!

Obedience to God's word is always a sure sign that one has come to personally know God in salvation

As we go on at 1 John 2, God now addresses another subject, which is obedience to His word, which is what characterizes all His children yet here on earth, as we now read at verses 3 to 6, "[3] **By this we know that we have come to know Him, if we keep His commandments. [4] The one who says, "I have come to know Him," and does not keep His commandments, is a liar, and the truth is not in him; [5] but whoever keeps His word, in him the love of God has truly been perfected. By this we know that we are in Him: [6] the one who says he abides in Him ought himself to walk in the same manner as He walked.**"

What all parents can testify to is that they all find it important that their children learn from the earliest age onward to obey them when they speak to them. Few parents ever bother to ask themselves why that is important, not realizing that if children do not obey their parents whom they do see, how will they obey God, Whom they do not see? God is testing children even while they are still children, which is why obedience to their parents is the only commandment He ever gives to them, noting what He tells them at Ephesians 6:1, "Children, obey your parents in the Lord, for this is right."

No parent expects their neighbor's kids to obey them. Why? Simply because they are not their kids. What this means then is that there is direct correlation between obedience and being one of the same family, which is why God says at 1 John 2:3, "By this we know that we have come to know Him, if we keep His commandments." In other words, a sure sign of one having come to know God in salvation is that one will be obeying Him, that is, carrying out His will as made known in His word, because He is our Father and we are His children! As we see at verse 4, God calls a liar every person who does not obey Him, yet claims to know Him, for to God, obedience is a sure sign of one being a true child of His!

Then we see that at 1 John 2:5 God adds, "but whoever keeps His word, in him the love of God has truly been perfected." What God is making known here is that to obey someone is also a sign of love for that person! Therefore, it one obeys God, then it means one loves God, which further means that one has truly come to personally know God in salvation, since the ability to love as He loves is one characteristic that God imparts to His own at the moment of one's salvation, noting what He tells us at Romans 5:5 in part, "…the love of God has been poured out within our hearts through the Holy Spirit who was given to us."

Then God concludes this section by saying at the end of 1 John 2:5 and at verse 6, "By this we know that we are in Him: [6] the one who says he abides in Him ought himself to walk in the same manner as He walked." In other words, we will know we have truly come to know God when we walk on earth as His own precious Son, The Lord Jesus Christ, walked while here on earth at His first coming from Heaven, which was in obedience to His Father's will, which was done as a pattern for us, noting what God tells us in this regard at Philippians 2:8 for instance, "Being found in appearance as a man, He humbled Himself by becoming obedient to the point of death, even death on a cross." In this way, The Son was not only being a Pattern for believers, but also showing His love for His Father.

Obedience to His Father was also the testimony God's Son gave for why He came to earth, noting John 6:38, "For I have come down from heaven, not to do My own will, but the will of Him who sent Me," with that will eventually leading Him to the cross. That is why God calls all believers, as His children yet on earth, to the same obedience at 1 John 2:6 and also at 1 Peter 2:21, "For you have been called for this purpose, since Christ also suffered for you, leaving you an example for you to follow in His steps…"

Love for those of the family of God is another sign that God gives for one truly having come to personally know Him in salvation

Then we are to see that God goes on to give another sign at 1 John 2:7-11 that will characterize those who have truly come to know Him in salvation, that is, who have truly been born anew spiritually into His family by The Holy Spirit, noting what we He now tells us through John, "[7] **Beloved, I am not writing a new commandment to you, but an old commandment which you have had from the beginning; the old commandment is the word which you have** heard. [8] **On the other hand, I am writing a new commandment to you, which is true in Him and in you, because the darkness is passing away and the true Light is already shining. [9] The one who says he is in the Light and yet hates his brother is in the darkness until now. [10] The one who loves his brother abides in the Light and there is no cause for stumbling in him. [11] But the one who hates his brother is in the darkness and walks in the darkness, and does not know where he is going because the darkness has blinded his eyes.**"

God begins at 1 John 2:7 here by letting us know that what He is writing about now, which is love for one another within the family of God, is not a new commandment, but one which He has been giving from the beginning. What God refers to as "the beginning" in this instance is from the time of His Son's public ministry on earth, when His Son told His disciples, those who were His followers on earth, what we read at John 13:34,35, "[34] A new commandment I give to you, that you love one another, even as I have loved you, that you also love one another. [35] By this all men will know that you are My disciples, if you have love for one another." As we can see from verse 35 here, a true disciple of God's Son, and by extension, one who has truly come to personally know God in salvation, is one who loves those who are part of the family of God!

Then when God goes on to say at 1 John 2:8 that He is giving "a new commandment," He is now referring to what He says at verse 9, namely, "The one who says he is in the Light and yet hates his brother is in the darkness until now." In other words, God is giving believers another clear sign about one who is a true child of God, which is whether one loves "his brother," which is "Adelphos" in the original, here indicating one who is a believer, as part of God's family. So the one who claims to be in the Light, that is, to be walking with God as His child, and yet does not love His brother, is a liar, and remains in spiritual darkness as yet, as all unbelievers do, since such a one has not yet come to personally know God in salvation! God then goes on to restate the same thing again at verse 10, now from the contrasting perspective, namely, "The one who loves his brother abides in the Light and there is no cause for stumbling in him."

What we see here then is that God has a way to test those who claim to be His children and yet are not, which should not surprise us, for generally speaking, no parent would accept children who might claim to be part of their family, when they are not. Today we have DNA tests to determine if a child is really that of a certain man or woman. In king Solomon's day in the Old Testament, God used a sword and wisdom in His servant to determine who was really the biological mother of the child which two women claimed was theirs (1 Kings 3:16-28).

God now addresses believers at three stages of the their spiritual growth

As we move on to verses 12 to 14 of 1 John 2, we notice that God now addresses three groups, which are believers at various stages of their spiritual growth in their walk with God while yet on earth, as we now read, "[12] **I am writing to you, little children, because your sins have been forgiven you for His name's sake. [13] I am writing to you, fathers, because you know Him who has been from the beginning. I am writing to you, young men, because you have overcome the evil one. I have written to you, children, because you know the Father. [14] I have written to you, fathers, because you know Him who has been from the beginning. I have written to you, young men, because you are strong, and the word of God abides in you, and you have overcome the evil one.**"

We note here first of all that God leads the apostle John to use various terms to address the believers he is writing to, these being "little children," "children," "young men," and "fathers." Secondly, we note that he addresses each group by saying the first time, "I am writing to you..." Then He again addresses the same groups, this time saying, "I have written to you." And thirdly, we are to notice here that the "children" of verse 2:13 refers to the same group as the "little children" of verse 2:12.

Therefore, in looking at what the apostle John is led of God to write to each group, we see an advance in spiritual growth being indicated. First then, we notice from verse 2:12 that we have the term "little children" mentioned, and what characterizes this group spiritually is that "your sins have been forgiven for His Name's sake." The term "little children" is one word in the original, that being "Teknion," meaning here one who is young or new in the faith. All who are believers in time need to pass through this stage, of having our sins forgiven as a work wholly of God's grace and power in salvation, as we see at Ephesians 2:8-10, which is why God adds here, "…for His Name's sake." We also note here that the term "little children" (Teknion) is used only by the apostle John in Scripture, once in the gospel account by John (at John 13:33) and seven times here at 1 John (at 1 John 2:1; 2:12; 2:28; 3:7; 3:18; 4:4; 5:21). What is interesting to note from its use at John 13:33 is that it is there applied by our precious Lord Jesus Christ to the eleven at the end of three and half years of walking with Him! This meant that these men were still spiritual babes in God's eyes even then!

What is important to note in each use of the term "little children" here at 1 John 2 is that in each case a very basic truth is being put forth, as what babes in the faith need to know. For instance, we note from 1 John 4:4 that these "little children" are there told, " You are from God, little children, and have overcome them; because greater is He who is in you than he who is in the world." What we are to see is that these "little children" have not overcome by anything they are presently doing, but rather here we are to see the truth that they are more than conquerors because they are from God, Who is in them as One greater than he (the devil) who is in the world.

And so, God begins here at verse 2:12 by saying to those who are "little children" in the faith, "your sins have been forgiven you for His name's sake." And if we recall the moment of our own salvation, that is the very first thing we did indeed experience, which is the forgiveness of all our sins ever committed against God since our childhood, which for some of us was like removing a mountain from our shoulders! And it was indeed for His own Name's sake that God did forgive us those sins at the moment of salvation, since we certainly did not deserve to be forgiven, but rather deserved eternal separation from God after physical death in a real place God calls "hell." It was for the eternal glory of God's own Name that He bestows salvation on unworthy sinners, because when we have finally entered God's Presence in Heaven, we will eternally be giving Him praise and thanksgiving, with adoration, forever and ever!

We are then to note that at verse 2:13b, God addresses the same group again and this time uses the word "children," which is "Paidion" in the original and again refers to those who are young in the faith. The apostle John uses this term only one other time, which is at 1

John 2:18. And what is said here, which additionally characterizes this same group, is that "you know The Father." This again is another first truth that we come to automatically say after realizing that our sins have been forgiven, which is that God is now our Father. The Holy Spirit in us is Who makes us realize this, as we see from Romans 8:15,16, "[15] For you have not received a spirit of slavery leading to fear again, but you have received The Spirit of adoption as sons by which we cry out, "Abba! Father!" [16] The Spirit Himself testifies with our spirit that we are children of God...," and also at Galatians 4:6, "Because you are sons, God has sent forth the Spirit of His Son into our hearts, crying, "Abba! Father!" The word "Abba" here is simply the same word "Father" in Aramaic, and is not what we would be led to say if our language of use is English.

Then pertaining to the next stage of spiritual growth, we note from 1 John 2:13,14 that the apostle John is led of God to refer to a second group called "young men." The term "young men" is also one word in the original, that being "Neaniskos," in reference to those who are a little older in the faith, having shown some spiritual growth. And what is said to characterize this group spiritually in God's sight is first that they have "overcome the evil one." In other words, this means that these have learned to walk by The precious Holy Spirit, as we see from Galatians 5:16, "But I say, walk by the Spirit, and you will not carry out the desire of the flesh." To have overcome the evil one, who is the devil, is to have learned to not give in to temptation, but instead to rely on the power of The precious Holy Spirit in our spirit to enable us to walk in newness of life in Christ Jesus, which is to live by God's imparted righteousness alone; which we automatically do as we walk with God with no known unconfessed sins in our lives!

We also need to note from 1 John 2:14 here that the apostle John is led to add something else about what characterizes the "young men" spiritually, when he is led to say, "you are strong, and the word of God abides in you, and you have overcome the evil one." Therefore we see that because this group, the young men, have learned to walk by The Holy Spirit, they are said to be strong in The Lord, and the word of God abides in them, because they also abide in the word of God, noting John 15:4-7. What is important to see and ever remember here is that for one to be able to do this is also wholly a work of God's grace and power alone!

And what also needs to be observed about the young men here is that once we have come to learn how to walk by The Holy Spirit daily – so as to not be walking by our sinful nature, but instead be walking by God's righteousness with no known unconfessed sins in our lives – is that God can then use us to reproduce ourselves spiritually! That is, we are then enabled of God to bear spiritual fruit, in that God is now able to save precious souls through us, as available vessels in His Hands. What would be useful here is noting what God's precious Son said to His disciples while on earth at John 15:4,5, "[4] Abide in Me, and I in you. As the branch cannot bear fruit of itself unless it abides in the vine, so neither can you unless you abide in Me. [5] I am the vine, you are the branches; he who abides in Me and I in him, he bears much fruit, for apart from Me you can do nothing."

Then we see from 1 John 2:13,14 that the third group that God addresses here are the "fathers," which is the word "Pater" in the original, meaning one regarded as spiritually mature. It is good to remember that none of these terms are meant in the physical sphere of life here, even though each of these terms have their equivalents in the physical realm. And what characterizes this group spiritually in God's sight is that "you know Him who has been from the beginning," repeated twice, at verse 2:13 then again at verse 2:14. What is important to note here is that The "Him Who has been from the beginning," is none else but God's precious Son, our Lord Jesus Christ, The Word made flesh. Therefore, this third group here are the fathers in the faith, those who are spiritually mature in God's sight, needing again to see this as wholly a work of God's grace and power alone!

So what is important to grasp here in regards to what characterizes this third group, the "fathers," is that they have gone through the previous stages of spiritual growth, that of "the little children" and "the young men," so that they have not only been walking with God moment by moment for many years, living only by His righteousness with no known unconfessed sins in their lives, God ever bearing fruit for His glory through them, but the fathers are also now shining examples for those who come after them in the faith! They are those who live on solid food of the word of God, noting what God says at Hebrews 5:14, " But solid food is for the mature, who because of practice have their senses trained to discern good and evil."

Those that God would characterize as "the fathers" have not only been used of God to reproduce themselves spiritually since young men, by leading others to personally know God in salvation through faith in our precious Lord Jesus Christ, noting what the apostle Paul says to the believers in Corinth at 1 Corinthians 4:14,15, "[14] I do not write these things to shame you, but to admonish you as my beloved children. [15] For if you were to have countless tutors in Christ, yet you would not have many fathers (Pater), for in Christ Jesus I became your father (where "became your father" is one word in the original and is used in the sense of the one giving the required seed for spiritual birth) through the gospel."

While this is true of "the fathers," we are also to see that they are committed to working with God while on earth, in the sense of being vessels in whom God can carry out His work! Let us note what God says here at 2 Corinthians 5:14,15 with 2 Corinthians 6:1, "[5:14] For the love of Christ controls us, having concluded this, that one died for all, therefore all died; [15] and He died for all, so that they who live might no longer live for themselves, but for Him who died and rose again on their behalf... [6:1] And working together with Him, we also urge you not to receive the grace of God in vain." So the grace of God upon "the fathers" is not "in vain," but rather is bearing fruit to the glory of God!

Therefore, we see here from 1 John 2:12-14 that God identifies for us three stages of spiritual growth that His own on earth will experience as a work of His grace and power alone after the initial moment of salvation. In the first, we have that stage of spiritual growth where we are as babes in the faith, simply little children, constantly under the watchful eye of God The Father, being yet in that tender stage of formation, noting Galatians 4:19. Then secondly, we have the next stage of spiritual growth, where the children develop into young men, learning to walk with increasing spiritual responsibility and develop some spiritual muscle, having been taught by God how to walk by The precious Holy Spirit, so as live by His righteousness alone, with no known unconfessed sins in one's life.

And thirdly, we have that last stage of spiritual growth, where the young men themselves become fathers, as those who have continued to grow in the knowledge and the grace of our precious Lord Jesus Christ (noting 2 Peter 3:18), and who have gone on to spiritual maturity, working with God while on earth so as to see His will accomplished on earth as it is in Heaven, having become intimately acquainted with God The Father through His Son, The Lord Jesus Christ, by The Holy Spirit through a moment by moment walk with God! Let us ever remember as we continue here that there are no shortcuts in the Christian life of a child of God while on earth! God has certain stages for His own to go through, same as there are in one physical's growth to maturity. Let us also always remember that in none of the terms being used here is God excluding female believers, since God always sees the female included in the male.

God's warning to His own yet on earth about the three sins that the devil likes to keep the whole of the human race in bondage to

As we continue at 1 John 2, we then note that God warns His own yet on earth about three sins in particular that the devil likes to keep the whole world of human beings in bondage to, which He now makes known at verses 2:15-17, "[15] **Do not love the world nor the things in the world. If anyone loves the world, the love of the Father is not in him.** [16] **For all that is in the world, the lust of the flesh and the lust of the eyes and the boastful pride of life, is not from the Father, but is from the world**. [17] **The world is passing away, and also its lusts; but the one who does the will of God lives forever**."

God introduces us to these three major sins experienced by the whole of the human race while one earth by first talking to believers about "the world" here at verse 2:15. The word "world," which God mentions six times in these three verses here is "Kosmos" in the original and refers to this present world system, which exists apart from God. In other words, it includes all unbelievers and the institutions of unbelievers on earth, including all "the things in the world," which are whatever pertains to unbelievers anywhere on earth.

What would be helpful here is looking at some verses of God's word, where He uses the word "world" in the same way as here, noting first what we read at John 3:17, "For God did not send the Son into the world (Kosmos) to judge the world, but that the world (Kosmos) might be saved through Him," and also at John 15:18,19, "[18] If the world (Kosmos) hates you, you know that it has hated Me (The Son) before it hated you. [19] If you were of the world (Kosmos), the world (Kosmos) would love its own; but because you are not of the world (Kosmos), but I chose you out of the world (Kosmos), because of this the world (Kosmos) hates you." As we see here, this present world of unbelievers, and all that pertains to them, hates God and believers, and therefore stands in opposition to God and all that is of Him!

And so that is why God says to believers yet on earth here what He does at verse 2:15, "Do not love the world nor the things in the world. If anyone loves the world, the love of the Father is not in him." There is no fence sitting with God, nor is there any compromise. We are either for God or we are against Him, which is why His Son said at Matthew 12:30 while on earth, "He who is not with Me is against Me; and he who does not gather with Me scatters." We either love God or else we love this world, there is no in between, as God makes clear at Matthew 6:24, "No one can serve two masters; for either he will hate the one and love the other, or he will be devoted to one and despise the other. You cannot serve God and wealth."

When God talks about "the love of the Father is not in him," He is speaking about the supernatural love of God that He imparts to us at salvation, when The Holy Spirit comes to indwell us, which we have seen mentioned at Romans 5:5 already. This supernatural love coming to us from God The Father through His Son by The Holy Spirit enables us to love God and all that pertains to God while we are on earth. Therefore, when we see a person professing to be a believer live in accordance with this world, which means one must then love this world, then God says to such a person, "the love of the Father is not in him," meaning that such a one is not a believer, that is, has not yet come to personally know God in salvation. Therefore, we see here that the love of the world is another test that God has in His arsenal to sift out those on earth claiming to be His when they are not!

And now that God has introduced believers to this world of unbelief, which stands in opposition to God and all that is of Him, He now goes on at 1 John 2:16 to introduce us to the three major sins that the god of this world, the devil, likes to use to keep human beings in bondage to him, when God now says, "For all that is in the world (Kosmos), the lust of the flesh and the lust of the eyes and the boastful pride of life, is not from the Father, but is from the world (Kosmos)."

Therefore, the three sins that God warns us about, which are not only part of this world, but are one of the main features of those who love this world, are: "The lust of the flesh and the lust of the eyes and the boastful pride of life..." These terms may not mean much to us until we realize that the three major sins God has in view here are lust, greed, and pride! These are like a cancer that touches all areas of life here on earth and brings death to life with God. These are three major sins which come from our sinful nature as human beings and which the devil likes to fan into flame whenever we are not careful and allow him some leeway into our lives, as for instance when we walk by our sinful nature.

And so, we need to see here that the word "lust" in the term "lust of the flesh" is "Epithumia" in the original and is the comprehensive term which God uses to refer to all manner of sinful desires, and we will see why in a moment. What we further need to see here is that the word "flesh" is the word "Sarx" in the original, which word pertains to some aspect of our bodies as human beings, which in this instance refers to the seat of our sinful nature, from which originates all those sinful desires that may come to a human being while here on earth.

And as already mentioned, since all human beings have a sinful nature, whether a believer or an unbeliever, then that means that all human beings can and do experience these desires coming from our sinful nature, which are sinful, since they are always in opposition to God's will for our lives. In other words, when we act out of our sinful nature, we are actually siding with the devil against God. Only The Holy Spirit, which believers receive at salvation, can keep our sinful nature under control (Galatians 5:22,23), which He does when we live by God's righteousness with no known unconfessed sins in our lives. Therefore, we can just refer to this first major sin here as 'lust.'

What would be helpful here is to see where God gives us some examples of this particular sin of lust, the first being the tenth of Gods Ten Commandments, which we see for instance at Exodus 20:17 in the Old Testament, where God warns all human beings, "You shall not covet your neighbor's house; you shall not covet your neighbor's wife or his male servant or his female servant or his ox or his donkey or anything that belongs to your neighbor." One New Testament example that God mentions here, out of many, is at 2 Timothy 2:22, where we read, "Now flee from youthful lusts (that is, sinful desires that are present in us since our youth) and pursue righteousness, faith, love and peace, with those who call on the Lord from a pure heart."

And as always here, God never leaves us without a remedy for our sinful nature, which, as already mentioned above, is The Holy Spirit in us as believers. Only He can keep that sinful nature under Divine control, as we read at Galatians 5:16, which we have already noted once before, "But I say, walk by the Spirit, and you will not carry out the desire (Epithumia) of the flesh (Sarx)." Then also at Romans 6:12,13, where God says to believers, "[12] Therefore do not let sin (the sinful nature) reign in your mortal body so that you obey its lusts (Epithumia), [13] and do not go on presenting the members of your body to sin (the sinful nature) as instruments of unrighteousness; but present yourselves to God as those alive from the dead, and your members as instruments of righteousness to God." So again, as we walk with God with no known unconfessed sins in our lives, God The Father, through His Son by The Holy Spirit, imparts to us His righteousness, which is His own righteous life for us to live by. And as long as we have no known unconfessed sins in our lives, we are living by God's righteousness, which further means we are not living by our sinful nature!

Then as to "the lust of the eyes," which God also mentions at 1 John 2:16, we are to see that the word "lust" is the same word "Epithumia," but here God relates it to the eyes, so that the major sin that is in view here is one we are also all familiar with, which is greed! And again, a couple of examples will suffice here in pointing out where God warns against this sin, first noting what we read at Ecclesiastes 4:8 in the Old Testament, "There was a certain man without a dependent, having neither a son nor a brother, yet there was no end to all his labor. Indeed, his eyes were not satisfied with riches and he never asked, "And for whom am I laboring and depriving myself of pleasure?" This too is vanity and it is a grievous task."

God then also warns us of this sin of greed at Luke 12:15-21, where He says, "[15] Then He said to them, "Beware, and be on your guard against every form of greed; for not even when one has an abundance does his life consist of his possessions." [16] And He told them a parable, saying, "The land of a rich man was very productive. [17] And he began reasoning to himself, saying, 'What shall I do, since I have no place to store my crops?' [18] Then he said, 'This is what I will do: I will tear down my barns and build larger ones, and there I will store all my grain and my goods. [19] And I will say to my soul, "Soul, you have many goods laid up for many years to come; take your ease, eat, drink and be merry." ' [20] But God said to him, 'You fool! This very night your soul is required of you; and now who will own what you have prepared?' [21] So is the man who stores up treasure for himself, and is not rich toward God."

Then we note that God goes on to warn believers at 1 John 2:16 about a third major sin that the devil likes to keep the whole of the human race in bondage to, which God refers to here as "the boastful pride of life." And as one can guess, the sin involved here is 'pride.' The words "boastful pride" is one word in the original Greek, which is "Alazoneia," and here refers to an arrogant display of bragging, where one trusts in his own power and resources, while shamefully despising and violating God's word. God gives us an example of this sinful display of pride at James 4:13-16, "[13] Come now, you who say, "Today or tomorrow we will go to such and such a city, and spend a year there and engage in business and make a profit." [14] Yet you do not know what your life will be like tomorrow. You are just a vapor that appears for a little while and then vanishes away. [15] Instead, you ought to say, "If the Lord wills, we will live and also do this or that." [16] But as it is, you boast in your arrogance (Alazoneia); all such boasting is evil."

What we can further say here as to why God points out these three sins of lust, greed, and pride that the whole human race is in bondage to apart from God is that we as believers are to be entirely in dependence on God in all areas of our lives, which is by God's design, so that He might be the Provider of all our needs! Therefore lust, greed, and pride, are stumbling blocks preventing us from truly depending on God alone for all we need for life here on earth. Therefore, lust has our desires focused on serving ourselves instead of God; while greed focuses us on seeking what God has not yet provided, being unwilling to wait on Him to provide, which He will if it is something we really need; and pride prevents us from walking in humbleness with God! All three sins leave God out entirely of our lives.

41

There is another very important truth that we need to take note of here, which is another reason why God brings up these three sins of lust, greed, and pride, that being first of all that these are the same three sins that Adam and Eve fell into temptation to when the devil came to tempt them in the garden of Eden, as we see at Genesis 3:6, adding verses 1 to 5 for context, "[1] Now the serpent was more crafty than any beast of the field which the Lord God had made. And he said to the woman, "Indeed, has God said, 'You shall not eat from any tree of the garden'?" [2] The woman said to the serpent, "From the fruit of the trees of the garden we may eat; [3] but from the fruit of the tree which is in the middle of the garden, God has said, 'You shall not eat from it or touch it, or you will die.' " [4] The serpent said to the woman, "You surely will not die! [5] For God knows that in the day you eat from it your eyes will be opened, and you will be like God, knowing good and evil." [6] When the woman saw that the tree was good for food (lust), and that it was a delight to the eyes (greed), and that the tree was desirable to make one wise (pride), she took from its fruit and ate; and she gave also to her husband with her, and he ate."

As we see at Genesis 3:6 here, our first parents, Adam and Eve, both fell into the temptations of the devil, which were lust, greed, and pride! And that this why, and this is the second aspect of this very important truth here, is that when God's precious Son, The Lord Jesus Christ, began His public ministry on earth, the very first thing that He did, after being baptized by John the Baptist to indicate that He was identifying with a sinful human race, was to face THE SAME THREE TEMPTATIONS OVER THE SAME THREE SINS OF LUST, GREED, AND PRIDE THAT ADAM AND EVE FACED AND TO NOW GAIN THE VICTORY OVER THOSE THREE SINS ON BEHALF OF THE HUMAN RACE!

And in order to see this, we need to turn to God's word to us at Matthew 4:1-11, and note what God there tells us, "[1] Then Jesus was led up by the Spirit into the wilderness TO BE TEMPTED BY THE DEVIL. [2] And after He had fasted forty days and forty nights, He then became hungry. [3] And the tempter came and said to Him, "If You are the Son of God, command that these stones become bread." [4] But He answered and said, "It is written, 'Man shall not live on bread alone, but on every word that proceeds out of the mouth of God.' " [5] Then the devil took Him into the holy city and had

Him stand on the pinnacle of the temple, [6] and said to Him, "If You are the Son of God, throw Yourself down; for it is written, 'He will command His angels concerning You'; and 'On their hands they will bear You up, so that You will not strike Your foot against a stone.' " [7] Jesus said to him, "On the other hand, it is written, 'You shall not put the Lord your God to the test.' " [8] Again, the devil took Him to a very high mountain and showed Him all the kingdoms of the world and their glory; [9] and he said to Him, "All these things I will give You, if You fall down and worship me." [10] Then Jesus said to him, "Go, Satan! For it is written, 'You shall worship the Lord your God, and serve Him only.' " [11] Then the devil left Him; and behold, angels came and began to minister to Him."

Later at 1 John 3:8, God tells us regarding His Son, giving us there one reason for why He came to the earth in our likeness, minus our sinful nature (since born of a virgin, in order not to incur our sinful nature, which comes through the male at conception), "the one who practices sin is of the devil; for the devil has sinned from the beginning. The Son of God appeared for this purpose, to destroy the works of the devil." And the way that God's Son goes about destroying the works of the devil is to first deal with the three temptations that the devil tempts all human beings with and win the victory over those temptations. The Lord Jesus Christ later dies on the cross bearing our sins in His own body on the cross (1 Peter 2:24) to provide His Father a basis for Him forgiving the sins of any sinner who believes in Him. So the victory over the three sins of lust, greed, and pride at the start of His public ministry culminates in His forever dealing with all sins forever in Himself on the cross!

How important then that we, as God's children yet on earth, always heed what He tells us at Mark 14:38, "Keep watching and praying that you may not come into temptation; the spirit is willing, but the flesh is weak," and also at 1 Peter 5:8, "Be of sober spirit, be on the alert. Your adversary, the devil, prowls around like a roaring lion, seeking someone to devour." And if we are not watching and praying, and living by The Holy Spirit, the devil will tempt us in one of these three areas of life - lust, greed, and pride! However, when we walk with God with no known unconfessed sins in our lives, we are being imparted His life to live by through His Son by His Holy Spirit in us, which means the devil then has no foothold into our lives! May this always be so, by God's marvelous grace and power. Amen.

So God concludes this section by saying at 1 John 2:17, "The world (Kosmos) is passing away, and also its lusts (Epithumia); but the one who does the will of God lives forever." The unbelievers of this world are all caught up in the affairs of this life, all seeking after things in a manner of life that is clearly anti-God and are all temporal. Believers, in contrast to this, should have one objective in life after coming to know God in salvation, which is to live for God's will. This is another test that God has for those to claim to be believers and are not, which is whether one does His will or not, for the reality is that only a believer will ever do the will of God, as we already noted.

Let us note some sobering thoughts from God here at Matthew 7:21, "Not everyone who says to Me, 'Lord, Lord,' will enter the kingdom of heaven, but he who does the will of My Father who is in heaven will enter," and also at 1 Peter 4:1,2, "[1] Therefore, since Christ has suffered in the flesh, arm yourselves also with the same purpose, because he who has suffered in the flesh has ceased from sin (that is, from living out of the sinful nature as the norm), [2] so as to live the rest of the time in the flesh no longer for the lusts of men, but for the will of God." If we claim to be followers of The Lord Jesus Christ, then we need to do, by God's grace and power, what He did while on earth, "For I have come down from heaven, not to do My own will, but the will of Him who sent Me" (John 6:38).

God now makes believers aware that it is "the last hour" of this present age, simply because "many antichrists have appeared"

As we turn to 1 John 2:18-25, God now wants to make believers aware that "the last hour" of the present third age of time has come, simply because "many antichrists have appeared" on the world scene, noting how He introduces this next section at 1 John 2:18-23 to begin with, "{18] **Children, it is the last hour; and just as you heard that antichrist is coming, even now many antichrists have appeared; from this we know that it is the last hour. [19] They went out from us, but they were not really of us; for if they had been of us, they would have remained with us; but they went out, so that it would be shown that they all are not of us. [20] But you have an anointing from the Holy One, and you all know. [21] I have not written to you because you do not know the truth, but because you do know it, and because no lie is of the truth. [22] Who is the liar but the one who denies that Jesus is the Christ?**

This is the antichrist, the one who denies the Father and the Son. [23] Whoever denies the Son does not have the Father; the one who confesses the Son has the Father also."

God is addressing believers here in the word "children," and wants to remind believers yet on earth at this present time that one can know that "the last hour" of this third age of time has come simply because "many antichrists have appeared." At this point, it is highly recommended that if one reading this is not familiar with the four ages of time, including the two separate comings from Heaven to earth of God's Son, The Lord Jesus Christ, then please take a moment here and read Addendum A and B at the back of the book before continuing, or else one will have difficulty comprehending much of what is being said in this present section.

And so, when God says "the last hour" here, He simply means that we know we are reaching the end of the present third age of time, simply because we are seeing "many antichrists" appear, which God defines for us at verse 2:22 when He says, "This is the antichrist, the one who denies the Father and the Son." Based on this statement, it is obvious that those who would be viewed as being labeled an "antichrist" here would be an unbeliever. But one might say here, 'Have we not had unbelievers since the time of God's Son on earth two thousand years ago?' In other words, the question is: Why is this being now characterized as the last hour? What we are to grasp here is that God is wanting to emphasize to believers that they will be able to recognize that the end of the present third age of time is approaching by the fact that there is a widespread denial of God The Father and His Son!

My latest book just published is titled, "This World's Return To Paganism Is Almost Complete!" The major theme of the book is that paganism is now in the process of replacing Christianity as the major influence on people's lives in all countries of the world. The reason that this is occurring is because the world needs to return to the same spiritual condition that it was in two thousand years ago when God's Son first came to earth. In other words, the world of the days into which Christianity made its entrance was dominated by paganism. And in God's design and plan for the ages, this world must return to the same darkness spiritually as it was in then, which was characterized by God The Father and The Son being unknown, before God resumes the second age of time to complete it with the last seven years remaining of it, and for His Son to return to earth again at the end of it. If one has not read Addendum A and B, one may have trouble understanding what has just been written.

That God is giving believers alive at the end of the present age a clue that the end of the age has come can be discerned from what God also says at 1 John 2:18, "just as you heard that antichrist is coming, even now many antichrists have appeared..." In other words, God mentions a person coming on the world scene, who is the "antichrist," who will himself deny both God The Father and The Son, which means that the fact that "many antichrists have appeared" indicates that the coming of the person who will be called the "antichrist" is not far away! When the person known as the "antichrist" appears on the world scene, he will lead the unbelievers of this world in opposition to God's Son and believers, which is why he will have the name "antichrist."

The words "antichrist" and "antichrists" are "Antichristos" in the original and occur only in the New Testament portion of the Bible, and then only in two of John's short letters, which are the focus of this book, that being at 1 John 2:18,22; 4:3; and 2 John 1:7. The person coming on the world scene, which God identifies at 1 John 2:18 with the name "antichrist," is elsewhere referred by other names in God's word. For instance, at 2 Thessalonians 2:3 God refers to this same person as "the man of lawlessness" and "the son of destruction." And let us note some brief description of him that God there gives at 2 Thessalonians 2:4,9, "[4] who opposes and exalts himself above every so-called god or object of worship, so that he takes his seat in the temple of God, displaying himself as being God... [9] that is, the one whose coming is in accord with the activity of Satan, with all power and signs and false wonders..."

Later in the God's book of Revelation, the person viewed here by God as being the antichrist at 1 John 2:18 is there at Revelation 13:1 referred to by God as being the "beast coming up out of the sea," and let us note here what God tells us about him at Revelation 13:6,7, "[6] And he opened his mouth in blasphemies against God, to blaspheme His name and His tabernacle, that is, those who dwell in heaven. [7] It was also given to him to make war with the saints and to overcome them, and authority over every tribe and people and tongue and nation was given to him." In the Old Testament, this person known as "the antichrist" is referred to by God as the "small horn" of Daniel 8:9, with God saying this of that small horn at Daniel 8:11, "It even magnified itself to be equal with the Commander of the host; and it removed the regular sacrifice from Him, and the place of His sanctuary was thrown down."

The only other truth that we need to remember here as believers living in "the last hour" of the present third age, which is fast coming to a close, is that this person God refers to as the "antichrist" at 1 John 2:18 is that he "is coming," with that coming being at the start of the seven years remaining of the second age of time, which begins immediately as this present third age ends, which God makes clear at 2 Thessalonians 2. If there is any person reading this who is not conversant with what is being talked about here, please refer to my book, "God's Second Letter To The Thessalonians," where this is dealt with in minute detail, since this is presently beyond the scope of the present book, apart from mentioning all this in passing.

Then we note that at 1 John 2:19 God makes another statement regarding the "many antichrists (who) have appeared," when He now says, "They went out from us, but they were not really of us; for if they had been of us, they would have remained with us; but they went out, so that it would be shown that they all are not of us." The "us," repeated five times here, needs to be seen as referring to believers on earth at this present time; while the "they," repeated six times here, is a reference to those unbelievers in the midst of believers, whom God characterized at verse 2:18 as "many antichrists have appeared." And what also needs to be grasped here is that God has the meeting of believers for worship in view here on The Lord's day, which is Sunday.

In other words, what God is making light of here is the fact that as this third age comes to a close, which is "the last hour" He has in view at 1 John 2:18, the unbelievers gathering with believers for Sunday worship will be seen as leaving from their midst. Why? For one, because "they were not really of us," in that they did not have a personal relationship with God in salvation, which means they were only professing to be believers. Only God can see the heart of a person, to know for sure those who are really His children on earth, as we read at 2 Timothy 2:19 in part, "Nevertheless, the firm foundation of God stands, having this seal, "The Lord knows those who are His…" "

And secondly, these unbelievers would now be leaving the midst of believers gathered to worship God simply because conditions in the world are such as this third age ends that the societies of the world have moved away from God! In other words, the pervasive spiritual darkness is such that unbelievers can now be identified as those who leave the gathering of believers, simply because only a true believer will continue to serve God and meet with His people in days where the majority of people are hostile to God The Father and His Son, as represented by Christianity in the last 2000 years! There will also be some 'churches,' so-called, right to the end of the present third age, but these will be unbelievers gathering with other unbelievers, where God is not even present. These will be part of the apostate church on earth during the last seven years of the second age, when the antichrist is ruling the world with the false prophet of Revelation 13:11, there referred to as "another beast coming up out of the earth," who will at that time be ruling over this world-encompassing apostate 'church.'

Then we note that at 1 John 2:20,21 God gives a contrast between unbelievers who do not know the truth and believes who do, when He says, "[20] But you have an anointing from the Holy One, and you all know. [21] I have not written to you because you do not know the truth, but because you do know it, and because no lie is of the truth." Believers know the truth here simply because they "have an anointing," in reference to The Holy Spirit that all believers receive at the moment of one's salvation, Who comes from "the Holy One," here speaking of God as now our Father. Being able to recognize the truth and know inwardly that it is the truth is yet another sign that God has for telling believers from unbelievers.

When God says here that believers "know the truth," He does not mean that we know all there is to know about God – for that is something that we will be learning for eternity to come – but rather, God here means that we all have the ability to grasp the truth due to The Holy Spirit being in our spirit to teach us the truth relating to God, as what we need to know in order to walk with Him and serve Him during our brief stay here. Let us note what God's Son tells us at John 14:26, "But the Helper, the Holy Spirit, whom the Father will

48

send in My name, He will teach you all things, and bring to your remembrance all that I said to you," and also at John 16:13, "But when He, the Spirit of truth, comes, He will guide you into all the truth; for He will not speak on His own initiative, but whatever He hears, He will speak; and He will disclose to you what is to come."

What God is also pointing out here is that believers would know the truth because the truth is from God, while lies come from the devil through unbelievers, whom they serve unknowingly, noting what God's Son said to unbelievers at John 8:44, "You are of your father the devil, and you want to do the desires of your father. He was a murderer from the beginning, and does not stand in the truth because there is no truth in him. Whenever he speaks a lie, he speaks from his own nature, for he is a liar and the father of lies." And so God adds here at 1 John 2:22a, "Who is the liar but the one who denies that Jesus is the Christ." To deny that "Jesus is the Christ," is to deny that God's eternally existing Son, Who is Christ, even before His Incarnation in human flesh, never took on the body prepared for Him by His Father (Hebrews 10:5) in the womb of the virgin and therefore was never born into this world with the name "Jesus."

The words "the Christ," which is "Ho Christos" in the original and refers to the fact that God's eternally existing Son, Who was The Christ before His incarnation in human flesh, is now Jesus Christ after His Incarnation into this world. Let us notice a couple of examples here to see this truth, first at Acts 17:2,3, "[2] And according to Paul's custom, he went to them (that is, the Jews in unbelief), and for three Sabbaths reasoned with them from the Scriptures, [3] explaining and giving evidence that the Christ had to suffer and rise again from the dead, and saying, "This Jesus whom I am proclaiming to you is the Christ," and also at Acts 18:5, "But when Silas and Timothy came down from Macedonia, Paul began devoting himself completely to the word, solemnly testifying to the Jews that Jesus was the Christ." So what the apostle Paul was doing was using the Old Testament Scriptures, which was all that was available to them at that time, and proving to the Jews that "the Christ" was indeed God's Son now come into the world in human flesh as "Jesus."

We then note that God ends this section with the two verses not yet quoted that being 1 John 2:24,25, which are addressed to believers, "[24] **As for you, let that abide in you which you heard from the beginning. If what you heard from the beginning abides in you, you also will abide in the Son and in the Father. [25] This is the promise which He Himself made to us: eternal life.**" What God means here by "what you heard from the beginning," repeated twice, is the truth that He has been teaching us by His Holy Spirit since the moment we came to personally know Him in salvation, which is when The Holy Spirit came to indwell in our human spirit. If that truth abides, that is, remains in us, in the sense of our living our lives by that truth, then what God assures us is that we too will then abide, that is, remain "in the Son and in the Father," which is by The Holy Spirit in us.

What God has in view here is related to what He said earlier at 1 John 1:3,6, only now using different words to express the same truth, namely that when we walk in the truth of God's word, we are in effect walking in fellowship with God The Father and His Son by The Holy Spirit. What this also means is that we are not living by our sinful nature when we do so, which further means that we are being imparted God's own righteousness, or righteous life, for us to live by moment by moment. That is why God adds here at verse 2:25, "This is the promise which He Himself made to us," who walk by God's word and not by our sinful natures, "eternal life," which is His own life being imparted to our spirit by The Holy Spirit moment by moment so that we might be enabled to walk with God here on earth!

God now concludes 1 John 2 with a final word of exhortation to believers

God, as our precious Father, wants His own children yet on earth not only to grow to spiritual maturity, but also to enjoy their daily walk with Him, so that it is a joy and not a burden for us, which is why God now closes with this word of exhortation, that is, of encouragement and comfort, to His own here at 1 John 2:26-29, "[26] **These things I have written to you concerning those who are trying to deceive you. [27] As for you, the anointing which you received from Him abides in you, and you have no need for anyone to teach you; but as His anointing teaches you about all things, and is true and is not a lie, and just as it has taught you, you abide in Him.**

[28] Now, little children, abide in Him, so that when He appears, we may have confidence and not shrink away from Him in shame at His coming. [29] If you know that He is righteous, you know that everyone also who practices righteousness is born of Him."

Twice here God encourages His own on earth, that is, believers, to "abide in Him," because God knows that the devil will try to deceive believers by all kinds of evil schemes that he has been using on the human race since Adam and Eve. And God also knows that our life with Him is by faith, where we constantly need to trust Him, even though we do not see Him, and to take Him at His word, which we do when we continue in the truth of His word.

God wants us to be found as walking with Him when His Son returns for us at the first stage of His second coming from Heaven to earth, which God mentions at verse 2:28 here in the words "when He appears," which is a reference to as for instance at 1 Thessalonians 4:14-17 and 2 Thessalonians 2:6,7. This "appearing" is the event taking place to end this present third age, when The Holy Spirit removes all believers from the earth to meet God's Son, The Lord Jesus Christ, just above the earth, which is when we have our sinful nature removed from us to enter Heaven, as God's eternal abode, with our new spiritual bodies to last forever.

And what is also needful here is for us to take a close look at what God tells us at 1 John 2:27 so as to not go astray, where God says, "As for you, the anointing which you received from Him abides in you, and you have no need for anyone to teach you; but as His anointing teaches you about all things, and is true and is not a lie, and just as it has taught you, you abide in Him." As was mentioned at verse 2:20 already, the "anointing," here repeated twice, is a reference to The Holy Spirit, indwelling the human spirit of every believer from the moment of one's salvation onward and forever. And since The Holy Spirit is in view here, the "it" that the translators have used here is not in the original and should be "He," since The Holy Spirit is Third Person of The Godhead, and is surely not an it!

And let us note what God tells believers at 1 Corinthians 2:11-13, in regards to The Holy Spirit's teaching us, "[11] For who among men knows the thoughts of a man except the spirit of the man which is in him? Even so the thoughts of God no one knows except the Spirit of

51

God. [12] Now we have received, not the spirit of the world, but the Spirit who is from God, so that we may know the things freely given to us by God, [13] which things we also speak, not in words taught by human wisdom, but in those taught by the Spirit, combining spiritual thoughts with spiritual words." Therefore, in this sense The precious Holy Spirit indeed is our Teacher, as The Lord Jesus Christ said He would be once He came to indwell us, noting John 14:26 again, "But the Helper, the Holy Spirit, whom the Father will send in My name, He will teach you all things, and bring to your remembrance all that I said to you."

And so, coming back to 1 John 2:27, we note that God also tells believers through the apostle John that "you have no need for anyone to teach you." And the obvious first question which arises here is: How about those Scripture verses which speak of human teachers? For instance, we read at 1 Timothy 3:2, "An overseer, then, must be above reproach, the husband of one wife, temperate, prudent, respectable, hospitable, able to teach...," and also at 2 Timothy 2:2, "The things which you have heard from me in the presence of many witnesses, entrust these to faithful men who will be able to teach others also."

It is clear from the first verse quoted here that elders, who are there in view, were to be able to teach God's people, which is of course in line with what God also tells us at Ephesians 4:11,12, "[11] And He gave some as apostles, and some as prophets, and some as evangelists, and some as pastors (the correct rendering here should be 'shepherds') and teachers, [12] for the equipping of the saints for the work of service, to the building up of the body of Christ..." And so we see that when gathered together as believers, the elders, who are the shepherd/teachers, are to equip the believers for the work of the ministry with the spiritual truth God leads them to impart for the spiritual growth of the body of believers in each local church. Therefore, we see from this that it was certainly God's will to have human teachers among His people. And not only that, but The Lord Jesus Christ Himself also did teach during His days on earth, noting what we read at Mark 9:31, "For He was teaching His disciples and telling them..."

What is clear then is that on one hand we have The Holy Spirit in us to teach us and on the other hand, God does raise men who are elders, whom He gifts as teachers to teach believers yet on earth. Therefore, the question we have now arrived at is: What is the relation between the teaching ministry of The Holy Spirit and that of God-raised human elders as teachers? To begin with here, we must note what God's precious Son was led of His Father to say at John 6:63, "It is the Spirit who gives life; the flesh profits nothing; the words that I have spoken to you are spirit and are life." In other words, The Lord Jesus Christ was always living in the fullness of The precious Holy Spirit, as One always led of Him (noting Luke 4:1,14), and therefore always speaking only what His precious Father was leading Him to say, which was spoken to Him by The precious Holy Spirit.

And here it would be helpful for us to note what God's Son said at John 14:24, "He who does not love Me does not keep My words; and the word which you hear is not Mine, but the Father's who sent Me," and also what was said of Him at John 3:34, "For He whom God has sent speaks the words of God; for He gives the Spirit without measure." What this means then is that every genuine human teacher must not only be raised of God (noting James 3:1,2 and 1 Timothy 1:6,7), but also one must be led of The Holy Spirit so as to speak what The precious Holy Spirit has led one to say, noting here what God says at 1 Peter 4,10,11, "[10] As each one has received a special gift, employ it in serving one another as good stewards of the manifold grace of God. [11] Whoever speaks, is to do so as one who is speaking the utterances of God; whoever serves is to do so as one who is serving by the strength which God supplies; so that in all things God may be glorified through Jesus Christ, to whom belongs the glory and dominion forever and ever. Amen." Therefore, any person not raised of God will not be Spirit-led and will not be teaching anything that comes from God, which will therefore not be useful for the growth of believers. As God's Son was led to say at John 7:18, "He who speaks from himself seeks his own glory; but He who is seeking the glory of the One who sent Him, He is true, and there is no unrighteousness in Him."

Therefore, coming back to 1 John 2:27, and the statement that "you have no need for anyone to teach you," we must now see that in a general context this is true, since each child of God is given The Holy Spirit at the moment of one's spiritual birth into God's family (noting also Ephesians 1:13,14), in order to be guided and taught of Him, as we have seen at John 14:26. However, we also need to see that a child of God who continues to live by The precious Holy Spirit after salvation, as is God's intention (noting Galatians 3:3 with 5:16), will gather with other believers in a local church, and there the elders, who are shepherd/teachers raised of God, will teach them, as men led of The Holy Spirit, to speak only what God leads them to say, as we saw at 1 Peter 4:11.

And so, just as the words The Lord Jesus Christ spoke, as given Him by God The Father, were taken by The Holy Spirit and applied to the hearts of the hearers as God determined, so too now (although not now under inspiration and very much subject to intervention by one's sinful nature) these shepherd/teachers will endeavor to speak only the words given them of God to speak, and that as being under the control of The Holy Spirit, Who will then take those words and apply them to the hearts of believers, as God determines. Therefore, we see that in this sense it is still The Holy Spirit Who is teaching believers, only doing so through a God-chosen and equipped human vessel. One does not have to go seeking human teachers. One only needs to live by The Holy Spirit and He will guide each believer into all the truth each believer needs in order to grow to spiritual maturity, whether directly through the written Word of God, and/or indirectly through God-raised and Spirit-filled shepherd/teachers!

Having already noted 1 John 2:28, in terms of God's Son coming to earth again, here having in view the first stage of His second coming, which is at the end of this present third age of time, God also further mentions in regards to that coming to earth again that if we continue to walk with Him, then when He does come, we will not be ashamed to meet Him! And then at 1 John 2:29, God ends the chapter by saying, "If you know that He is righteous, you know that everyone also who practices righteousness is born of Him." To say that God is "righteous" here simply means that all He thinks, all He does, and all He says is right, which further means that the life He lives is not only eternal life, since He is an eternal Being, but it is also righteous, that is, perfect righteousness.

So we see God give another sign here for one who would be regarded as a true believer, in "that everyone also who practices righteousness is born of Him." In other words, as mentioned numerous times already since the beginning of the book, if we are living moment by moment with no known unconfessed sins in our lives, then we are automatically living by The precious Holy Spirit, which further means that we are automatically being imparted God's righteous life, or righteousness, to live by, so that we may walk with God moment by moment carrying out His will for our lives! What has just been written is what God means when he says "who practices righteousness." We will have more to say about this in the next chapter.

CHAPTER THREE

1 John 3:1-24

The fact that believers are the only children God has on earth brings a unique responsibility

As we begin 1 John 3, we note that God makes light of the truth that believers are His own children yet on earth, which fact brings a unique responsibility, as God now makes clear at verses 3:1-3, where He says to believers, "[1] **See how great a love the Father has bestowed on us, that we would be called children of God; and such we are. For this reason the world does not know us, because it did not know Him. [2] Beloved, now we are children of God, and it has not appeared as yet what we will be. We know that when He appears, we will be like Him, because we will see Him just as He is. [3] And everyone who has this hope fixed on Him purifies himself, just as He is pure**."

Believers probably do not very often dwell on the truth that they are called "the children of God," and that by God Himself! What God wants believers to be aware of here is that this fact should make us realize just how much God loves us, who are believers! Just think about this for a moment, God, Who is eternally existing, Who created all that exists of what is good, and Who is absolute perfection in every way in His Persons of Father, Son, and Holy Spirit, so that all He thinks, says, and does is perfect; that God loves us, who are but a handful of dust and who sin far too easily when not undergirded and protected by Him! How we need to be reminded over and over again that is was God's love for us that led Him to come for us while we were yet sinners.

And how much we need to ever remember that it was God's love for the human race that led Him to give up His Son in the first place, in order that He might come to earth to take on our humanity (John 3:16 with Hebrew 10:5), and that it was The Son of God's love for us that led Him to give Himself up unto death in payment for our sins at the cross, that the barrier of sin separating human beings from God might be removed, so that human beings might then have a basis for coming to personally know God (1 John 3:16 with 1 Peter 3:18). So let those words sink into our minds and our hearts, which God speaks here at 1 John 3:1, when He says, "See how great a love the Father has bestowed on us…" Being called "children of God" now is but the end result of all that God in love has already bestowed on us!

And God continues at 1 John 3:1b here and says that it is because believers are the very children of God on earth now that "the world (Kosmos) does not know us," that is, that world system still in unbelief, with all its institutions and systems, does not know believers, simply because they do not know God. Let us note what God's Son said to His followers one day while on earth at John 15:19, which is applicable to believers now also, "If you were of the world (Kosmos, and so in all five occurrences here), the world would love its own; but because you are not of the world, but I chose you out of the world, because of this the world hates you." What we need to see here is that from the moment of our salvation onward, we have been transferred by God from the devil's domain and brought into God's Kingdom, which renders us eternally united, and so identified, with God, noting what God tells us at Colossians 1:12-14, "[12] giving thanks to the Father, who has qualified us to share in the inheritance of the saints in Light. [13] For He rescued us from the domain of darkness, and transferred us to the kingdom of His beloved Son, [14] in whom we have redemption, the forgiveness of sins."

When God goes on and says at 1 John 3:2, "Beloved, now we are children of God, and it has not appeared as yet what we will be. We know that when He appears, we will be like Him, because we will see Him just as He is," He there says two things we know for sure. One is that we are children of God, and two is that when God's precious Son, The Lord Jesus Christ, appears again at the end of this present third age, which is the time of glorification for believers of this present time, then we will all be changed into the image of God's Son in an instant, with our sinful nature removed from us and our bodies changed into spiritual bodies so that they will now last forever in Heaven, where we will be forever with God.

This will be so for us as believers simply because this was so for God's Son, Who is a Pattern for not only our present life now on earth, but also for all eternity in Heaven. Let us note what God tells us in this regard at Romans 8:29,30, "[29] For those whom He foreknew, He also predestined to become conformed to the image of His Son, so that He would be the firstborn among many brethren; [30] and these whom He predestined, He also called; and these whom He called, He also justified; and these whom He justified, He also glorified." Here God sees believers from eternity past until each is in Heaven with Him at glorification, even though this has not yet taken place for all believers of time, only for those of the first age. And so, before time began, God knew us as His own because that is when He first chose us for Himself out of all human beings freely rejecting Him, and it was then that He predestined us to become His through salvation in time. Then when time began with His original creation of all things, including angelic beings and human beings, God called and justified (that is, brought salvation to) all those whom He had foreknown and predestined in eternity past. And then the believers of each of the four ages of time are brought to Heaven through glorification each at their proper time and order.

Coming back to 1 John 3:2, we then see that the only thing we do not know is "what we will be." What God is making reference to here is our new spiritual bodies, which we will have in glorification. We do know that these bodies will be like that of God's Son, The Lord Jesus Christ, now glorified, which is a spiritual body, noting what God tells us at 1 Corinthians 15:42-44,49, "[42] So also is the resurrection of the dead (which is a reference to the time of glorification for believers). It is sown a perishable body, it is raised an imperishable body; [43] it is sown in dishonor, it is raised in glory; it is sown in weakness, it is raised in power; [44] it is sown a natural body, it is raised a spiritual body. If there is a natural body, there is also a spiritual body... [49] Just as we have borne the image of the earthy, we will also bear the image of the heavenly."

And so again here, we are to see that we will have a spiritual body in resurrection, because God's Son now has, and we will be like Him in terms of now sinless forever due to our sinful nature having now been removed from us. However, since God has never given us a picture of what His precious Son looks like, which is why He forbids making any graven image of Him (Exodus 20:4), then that is also true of us, in that we will not know what we will look like until that time of glorification occurs. God is saying here that He will not disclose that to us until then.

One thing that I personally believe here is that we will all be around 33 years of age in glorification, since that is the age God's Son was at when He was glorified after His being raised from the dead the third day. And this is likely the age that Adam and Eve were at when first created by God, because thirty-three years of age refers to one who is fully grown in every way, physically, emotionally, and mentally. What this means then is that there are no babies, young children, or seniors in Heaven, but we will all be like the angels (Luke 20:34-36), neither male nor female, having only what is required in order to exist in that spiritual realm. For instance, we will no longer have a stomach and elimination system, as there will be nothing physical of nature there (1 Corinthians 6:13). God is a spirit Being (John 4:24), the angel are spirit beings, and Heaven is a spiritual place, which means that we too will therefore become spiritual beings fitted for that very real place forever!

And now based on all God has prepared for believers for both time and eternity, this brings a responsibility, as God makes clear at 1 John 3:3, "And everyone who has this hope fixed on Him purifies himself, just as He is pure." When God speaks of "this hope fixed on Him" here, He is making reference to what awaits us past the grave. That is our hope, to experience all that His own precious Son experienced Himself as He went before us, noting what God says at 2 Corinthians 4:14, "knowing that He (God The Father) who raised the Lord Jesus will raise us also with Jesus (at the first stage of His second coming) and will present us with you."

Since the hope of every believer of time is life with God past the grave, then all believers of every age of time has the same responsibility toward God, which is that "everyone... purifies himself, just as He is pure." In other words, knowing that we will all one day soon have the same image as God's Son forever, Who is sinless, then we too need to start now in being pure, which is without known unconfessed sins in our lives, which is what "being pure" means here. Keeping ourselves pure as believers while yet on earth will now be the subject matter that God addresses in the next section that we will be looking at 1 John 3:4-10.

Before we came to know God in salvation, we were unbelievers practicing sin; and now that we are the children of God, we as believers are to practice only righteousness while on earth!

As mentioned above, God now goes on in this section to greatly expand on the subject of believers keeping themselves in purity while on earth in light of their not only being the children of God, but also in light of the hope of seeing God and being with Him forever once our time of glorification occurs past the grave. And this is what God now makes reference to when He says at 1 John 3:4-10 that believers need to practice righteousness after salvation, and no longer practice sin, which is all we ever did when we were unbelievers, noting what we there read, "**[4] Everyone who practices sin also practices lawlessness; and sin is lawlessness. [5] You know that He appeared in order to take away sins; and in Him there is no sin. [6] No one who abides in Him sins; no one who sins has seen Him or knows Him. [7] Little children, make sure no one deceives you; the one who practices righteousness is righteous, just as He is righteous; [8] the one who practices sin is of the devil; for the devil has sinned from the beginning. The Son of God appeared for this purpose, to destroy the works of the devil. [9] No one who is born of God practices sin, because His seed abides in him; and he cannot sin, because he is born of God. [10] By this the children of God and the children of the devil are obvious: anyone who does not practice righteousness is not of God, nor the one who does not love his brother.**"

And in order not to go astray in our thinking here, it is very important at the outset that we know what God means when He speaks at 1 John 3:4 of those who 'practice sin.' First then, the word "practice" is "Poieo" in every occurrence here, which has reference to what is habitual in the life of a person. And so, for unbelievers what is habitual, that is, continually seen from their lives, is the practice of sin, since unbelievers are always living by their sinful nature, which therefore means that everything coming from that nature, in terms of thoughts, acts, and words, is an act of sin. And secondly, when God speaks of "lawlessness" here, which is "Anomia" in the original, He is speaking of those who habitually live their lives in the rejection of the law of God, and therefore the will of God for their lives, as made known in the word of God. All unbelievers do so, in terms of practicing lawlessness, due to living by the flesh, not having The Holy Spirit to give them the life of God to live by, which means they live only for themselves while on earth, noting also what God says of them at Romans 8:7, "...the mind set on the flesh is hostile toward God; for it does not subject itself to the law of God, for it is not even able to do so..."

And to ensure that believers do not follow the same path after salvation as before salvation, God reminds believers here at 1 John 3:5, "You know that He appeared in order to take away sins; and in Him there is no sin." In other words, God's Son, The Lord Jesus Christ, has specifically been given by The Father to bear our sins in His own body on the cross in order to "take away sins," so how can we willingly go on sinning after salvation? As God says at Hebrews 9:26 in part, "...but now once at the consummation of the ages He has been manifested to put away sin by the sacrifice of Himself." The penalty for sin is death (Romans 6:23), which God's Son willingly suffered on behalf of the human race in order to bring us to God, as we see at 1 Peter 3:18 in part, "For Christ also died for sins once for all, the just for the unjust, so that He might bring us to God..."

The death of God's Son on behalf of a sinful human race made it possible for those whom God saves in time to have their sins forgiven at the moment of salvation and afterwards, so that one can live a pure life with God after salvation, which one does live when one has no known unconfessed sins in one's life. After all, "in Him," that is, in God's Son, "there is no sin," in terms of there not only never having been an act of sin, but also never having had a sinful nature. God, and therefore also His Son, is impeccable, which means He is not even able to sin. We as human beings, because we all have a sinful nature, even after salvation, are able to do what God cannot ever do, which is sin! But the point that God is making here in telling us that "in Him there is no sin" is to secure the same desire from believers after salvation, seeing that we are not only united with God's Son spiritually by The Holy Spirit now (1 Corinthians 12:13,27), but we are also to walk with God daily, Who is in the light, which means that we need to continually be without known unconfessed sins in our lives in order to be able to do so.

And so that is why God goes on now at 1 John 3:6 and adds, "No one who abides in Him sins; no one who sins has seen Him or knows Him." In other words, it is inconsistent for a believer who wants to walk with God to want to go on sinning after salvation. What is critical to see here is that God has the 'practice of sin' in view in the word "sins," repeated twice here. The reality, as we have seen, is that even believers sin after salvation, and so we need to see verse 3:6 as follows, "No one who abides in Him sins (that is, practices sin); no one who sins (practices sin) has seen Him or knows Him." This is clear from what God adds at verse 3:9 here, "No one who is born of God (spiritually) practices sin, because His seed (The Holy Spirit) abides in him; and he cannot (practice) sin, because he is born of God."

Only unbelievers will 'practice sin,' as we have noted. Believers cannot 'practice sin,' since the word 'practice' here refers to what is continual or habitual in the life of a person. Because a believer has The Holy Spirit indwelling in one's spirit, then one will be immediately convicted of sin at the moment a sin – any sin – is committed, so that one who is a believer immediately experiences the loss of God's peace and joy, including the impartation of God's life to live by until that sin is confessed to God, as we have seen when looking at 1 John 1:9. Same as a person cannot go back to a mother's womb after being born physically into this world, so likewise, God says it is impossible for a child of His who has been born spiritually, that is, of The Holy Spirit into God's family, to go back to practicing sin, which was one's condition before salvation!

Years ago, I remember sitting down with a Christian friend of mine, and while we were talking, he related the fact that two neighbors of his, who he said were Christians, had recently lost their spouses and had started living together. I immediately went to this passage in 1 John 3:4-10 to point out that it is impossible for a child of God to 'practice sin,' as only unbelievers will ever do so. For instance, a child of God is continually being tempted by the devil to act out of one's sinful nature, which results in a sin being committed against God if one gives in to that temptation. Then due to God's conviction, as just mentioned above, one who is a child of God will confess that sin and God will immediately forgive the sin and restore His child to a walk with Him based on the truth that God's Son has already paid the penalty of death for that sin and all sins, when He died for us at the cross. So if we see someone claiming to be a believer and practicing sin, then we can be sure that such a person is as yet an unbeliever. And so, the 'practice of sin' is yet another way that God can tell as a visible sign that one is a child of His or not!

What has just been said above is made even clearer by God when He then goes on to add at 1 John 3:7,8a, "[7] Little children, make sure no one deceives you; the one who practices righteousness is righteous, just as He is righteous; [8a] the one who practices sin is of the devil; for the devil has sinned from the beginning." Here we see that God has again the contrast between believers and unbelievers in view. And so, on the one hand we have believers, as the ones "who practices righteousness" being as God is, which is "righteous," and therefore a believer; simply because one is living by God's own life, that is, by His righteousness being imparted moment by moment by The Holy Spirit as one walks with God with no known unconfessed sins in one's life. Then on the other hand, we have unbelievers, as those "who practices sin," noting carefully here that God says these are "of the devil," simply because all unbelievers are yet part of the domain of that evil one, generally unknowingly serving him by always practicing sin, because only ever living by their sinful nature.

And before going further here, and in order to spare believers from some possible confusion, we are to note that at Romans 7:15 God uses the word "practicing," and at Romans 7:19 the word "practice," in relation to believers, but there those words are different Greek words in the original, being "Prasso," and not the word "Poieo," as here at 1 John 3:4-10. A less confusing rendering would have been the words "doing" and "do" instead, noting here what we read at Romans 7:14-19, which is also instructive for our present subject matter, "[14] For we know that the Law (God's word) is spiritual, but I am of flesh, sold into bondage to sin (the sinful nature). [15] For what I am doing, I do not understand; for I am not practicing ("Prasso," that is, 'not doing') what I would like to do, but I am doing the very thing I hate. [16] But if I do the very thing I do not want to do, I agree with the Law (God's word), confessing that the Law is good. [17] So now, no longer am I the one doing it, but sin (my sinful nature) which dwells in me. [18] For I know that nothing good dwells in me, that is, in my flesh; for the willing is present in me, but the doing of the good is not. [19] For the good that I want, I do not do, but I practice ("Prasso," that is, 'do') the very evil that I do not want."

God then goes on to say here that the devil "has sinned from the beginning," in reference to the fact that after being created as an angelic being by God with no sin at the time of the original creation, this angelic being sinned the original sin against God and became the devil, with the proper name of Satan, which was at some point between the start of Genesis 2 and the start of Genesis 3 in time. Let us note what God says of unbelievers and of the devil at John 8:44, "You are of your father the devil, and you want to do the desires of your father. He was a murderer from the beginning, and does not stand in the truth because there is no truth in him. Whenever he speaks a lie, he speaks from his own nature, for he is a liar and the father of lies." Here we see that the devil can only act "from his own nature," which is true of all unbelievers, which nature is sinful.

However, this is not to be so for believers after salvation, in terms of again acting out of one's sinful nature. God gives us another reason why at 1 John 8b, "The Son of God appeared for this purpose, to destroy the works of the devil." The question that might arise here is: What are the works of the devil that God's Son has come on earth to destroy? God introduces us to the works of the devil when He says at Romans 5:12, "Therefore, just as through one man (Adam) sin entered into the world, and death through sin, and so death spread to all men, because all sinned…" And we have seen already from Genesis 3:1-6 that it was the devil who led Adam and Eve into sin, after he himself as now a fallen angelic being had committed the original sin to enter God perfect and sinless creation. And since death is the end result of sin, and with all human beings having been infected by it from the sinful nature passed on from male to female to offspring since the time of Adam, then that means that the devil is also responsible for death having entered God's creation, which is why God says of death in relation to the devil at Hebrews 2:14, "Therefore, since the children share in flesh and blood, He Himself (God's Son) likewise also partook of the same, that through death He might render powerless him who had the power of death, that is, the devil."

Therefore, the two works of the devil that God's Son, The Lord Jesus Christ, came to earth in the likeness of human flesh to destroy are sin and death! The first work of the devil that God's Son then destroyed was sin, when He died on the cross for the sin of all mankind, making it possible for human beings to live a pure life with God on earth, as

God intended at original creation when He made the whole human race sinless when first created. Then after being buried, God The Father raised His Son from the dead the third day, which means that through His resurrection from the dead, He won the victory over death, in that it can be abolished by God. In other words, because God's Son was raised from the dead, God can likewise raise all human beings from the dead after death in order to remove death forever from His sight! That is why God says at Acts 2:24 in this regard, "But God raised Him (His Son) up again, putting an end to the agony of death, since it was impossible for Him to be held in its power," since He was The Son of God, Who is eternal.

Two passages of God's word, which would be helpful to note here in this regard to the resurrection from the dead, are first at Acts 24:14,15, "[14] But this I (the apostle Paul) admit to you, that according to the Way which they call a sect I do serve the God of our fathers, believing everything that is in accordance with the Law and that is written in the Prophets; [15] having a hope in God, which these men cherish themselves, that there shall certainly be a resurrection (from the dead) of both the righteous and the wicked." And the other passage we need to note is what God says about sin and death, and its elimination, at 1 Corinthians 15:53-57, "[53] For this perishable (speaking of our physical human body) must put on the imperishable, and this mortal must put on immortality. [54] But when this perishable will have put on the imperishable, and this mortal will have put on immortality, then will come about the saying that is written, "Death is swallowed up in victory. [55] "O death, where is your victory? O death, where is your sting?" [56] The sting of death is sin, and the power of sin is the law; [57] but thanks be to God, who gives us the victory through our Lord Jesus Christ."

Since both works of the devil, namely sin and death, are removed in time through the death, burial, and resurrection from the dead of God's Son in human flesh, The Lord Jesus Christ; then that is why this is the gospel, that is, the good news that God has for every human being born into this world in time, which one must believe in order to have the forgiveness of sins and eternal life with God, so as to now be free to serve God in purity and also be free of the fear of death due to now having eternal life with God. That believing the gospel is the requirement for salvation is made clear by what God says at 1 Corinthians 15:1-4, "[1] Now I make known to you, brethren, the gospel which I preached to you, which also you received, in which also you stand, [2] by which also you are saved, if you hold fast the word which I preached to you, unless you believed in vain. [3] For I delivered to you as of first importance what I also received, that Christ died for our sins according to the Scriptures, [4] and that He was buried, and that He was raised on the third day according to the Scriptures."

What this means then is that if any human being believes the gospel, all of one's sins committed since the age of accountability as a child are forgiven and one receives God's own life to live by, due to The Holy Spirit having come to indwell in one's human spirit to impart that life, which is eternal life. And so, let us note 1 John 3:9 again here, before going on to close this section, "No one who is born of God practices sin, because His seed (The Holy Spirit) abides in him; and he cannot sin, because he is born of God." This should be clear enough to every person who reads this, namely that no child of God will continue to sin without a confession of sin being made directly to God after an act of sin, as we have seen at 1 John 1:9. As already mentioned, this is another sign that God has for determining whether a person claiming to be a child of God really is or not, in terms of whether one practices sin or not!

Then God closes this section by saying at 1 John 3:10, "By this the children of God and the children of the devil are obvious: anyone who does not practice righteousness (but instead practices sin) is not of God, nor the one who does not love his brother." In other words, the children of God on earth will be characterized by those who live by God's righteousness, that is, by God's own imparted life automatically imparted to one's spirit as one walks with God with no known unconfessed sins in one's life! And the children of the devil, as those still part of his domain and under his control, are all those who do not practice that righteousness, but instead practice what their father the devil practices, which is sin continually. Such a person is not of God, with God adding in closing, "nor the one who does not love his brother," which God adds here in order to introduce the next section. But let us also recall that this is theme that God has already touched upon at 1 John 2:9-11, namely that one who claims to be a child of God will love his brother, as those who are part of the family of God!

God gives further proof that love for those of the family of God is a sign that one is a believer

Having introduced this present section at the end of 1 John 3:10 by saying that "one who does not love his brother," as part of the family of God, is not a believer, that is, a child of God; God now goes on at 1 John 3:11-15 on that same theme, now giving further proof that love for the family of God is a sure sign that one is a child of His, noting what we there read, "[11] **For this is the message which you have heard from the beginning, that we should love one another**; [12] **not as Cain, who was of the evil one and slew his brother. And for what reason did he slay him? Because his deeds were evil, and his brother's were righteous.** [13] **Do not be surprised, brethren, if the world hates you.** [14] **We know that we have passed out of death into life, because we love the brethren. He who does not love abides in death.** [15] **Everyone who hates his brother is a murderer; and you know that no murderer has eternal life abiding in him.**"

As already mentioned, this is a theme that God earlier dealt with at 1 John 2:9-11, there having dealt with the subject in relation to those who are in the Light in contrast to those who are yet in the darkness. And so, when God says here at 1 John 3:11 that "this is the message which you have heard from the beginning," He is referring to the start of when we first came to know God in salvation, that is when we would have heard the truth "that we should love one another," as those who are of the same family of God. This is a truth that God Himself would have taught us by His Holy Spirit coming to indwell us, since in coming to indwell us, The Holy Spirit would have cleansed our hearts of all sin, filled our lives with God's life, which is eternal, and would have filled our hearts with God's love (Romans 5:5). And in now having God's love filling our hearts, that love would first be directing our hearts to God Himself, to love Him as He had loved us in salvation, and then our hearts would be directed to those of the family of God that we came in contact with, that we might be enabled by God's Spirit in us to love them as we love ourselves!

God then gives the example of Cain (noting Genesis 4:1-8) here at 1 John 3:12, as one who did not have this love of God in his heart toward his brother Abel, who was a believer; simply because Cain was not a child of God, but rather a child of the devil. That is why he killed his brother, because the devil is a murderer from the beginning and Cain was following the example of his father (John 8:44). Since Abel was a believer, and the devil hates believers, because he hates God and all those who belong to Him, then Cain, who was a child of the devil, hated his brother Abel simply because his brother was a child of God. That is why God goes on at 1 John 3:13 and says to believers, "Do not be surprised, brethren, if the world (Kosmos) hates you," simply because the world, as we have seen, is under the control of the evil one (1 John 5:19), which will, with all unbelievers in it, be hating believers, because they belong to God, while they belong to the devil (1 John 3:10).

At 1 John 3:14, God goes on and says that "we know that we have passed out of death into life, because we love the brethren. He who does not love abides in death." Therefore, a sure sign that one has been born into God's family through a spiritual birth when The Holy Spirit came to indwell our human spirit is the fact that "we love the brethren," with the love that God poured into our hearts when He gave us His Holy Spirit at salvation. And so, the truth that believers "have passed out of death into life," simply means that we have passed from a state of being dead to a life with God, having previously been in such a state due to being children of the devil (noting Ephesians 2:1-3), but now we have passed from that into a state of life with God, when we received The Holy Spirit at the moment of believing the gospel, which was the moment of our salvation. Unbelievers still remain in that state of death to life with God, because like the devil and the world, they do not have the love of God in their hearts to love God and those who belong to Him!

This is made clearer still at 1 John 3:15 when God says plainly, "Everyone who hates his brother is a murderer; and you know that no murderer has eternal life abiding in him." What God wants to make people aware of here is that there is a real danger among unbelievers, who do not have the love of God in their hearts due to not having The Holy Spirit, which means that like the devil they not only hate believers, but they are also murderers like him, as was the case with the example of Cain which God gave. In other words, what God is pointing out here is that the direct opposite of love is hate, and once hatred for another person has set in, then the end result of that hatred is murder! That this is the case can be seen from what God's Son said at Matthew 5:21-24 one day while teaching about the sixth of the Ten Commandments of God, as we there read, "[21] You have heard that the ancients were told, 'You shall not commit murder' and 'Whoever commits murder shall be liable to the court.' [22] But I say to you that everyone who is angry with his brother shall be guilty before the court; and whoever says to his brother, 'You good-for-nothing,' shall be guilty before the supreme court; and whoever says, 'You fool,' shall be guilty enough to go into the fiery hell. [23] Therefore if you are presenting your offering at the altar, and there remember that your brother has something against you, [24] leave your offering there before the altar and go; first be reconciled to your brother, and then come and present your offering."

What we see from this passage is a progression in one's feelings toward another human being, which starts with anger, develops into hatred, and ends in murder! So God warns people to deal with their anger so as not to let it develop into hatred, with only God knowing what the end result would then be. All of this is mentioned here to point out the gravity of not loving another human being, which is what will characterize unbelievers. God calls such here "a murderer," since that is the end result of what hatred leads to. And so, God's conclusion here is that "you know that no murderer has eternal life abiding in him," simply because those who have eternal life are believers who are filled with the love of God for those of the family of God through the love imparted by The Holy Spirit from the moment of one's salvation onwards. Unbelievers do not have The Holy Spirit, or the love of God in them, with God seeing them in their final state of what they can become due to this fact, which "is a murderer."

God gives a practical example of love in action that He wants His own children on earth to display

In case someone had not noticed, God is a very practical God! How do we know that? Well, the answer is that one of the reasons that His Son spent three and half years of His life in public ministry on earth, which means that it could be observed by one and all, including having given us not one, but four accounts of that public life on earth (namely Matthew, Mark, Luke, and John), is that His Son might be a Pattern for the kind of life that God wants all of His children on earth to display. And so, at 1 John 11:16-18 here, God gives us a practical example, as something even His own Son, The Lord Jesus Christ, did Himself while on earth, "[16] **We know love by this, that He laid**

70

down His life for us; and we ought to lay down our lives for the brethren. [17] But whoever has the world's goods, and sees his brother in need and closes his heart against him, how does the love of God abide in him? [18] Little children, let us not love with word or with tongue, but in deed and truth."

The love in action that God's precious Son displayed on behalf of all human beings while on earth was "that He laid down His life for us," when He died on the cross, bearing there the penalty due our sins. At John 3:16, we read that "God so loved the world (Kosmos) that He gave His only begotten Son…," and now God's Son shows the fullest extent of God's love for the human race in dying a death He did not deserve, since He was sinless. Based on that practical display of the love of God here, God says to believers "we ought to lay down our lives for the brethren," that is, for those who are of the family of God. And since God knows that the death of His Son at the cross on behalf of the whole human race is a unique event that never needs repeating, He therefore gives a practical example of how believers can put their love for one another into practice when He says here at 1 John 3:17, "whoever has the world's goods, and sees his brother in need," one is not to close "his heart against him," but rather one is to meet that need in accordance to what one has, and that as a cheerful giver (noting 2 Corinthians 8,9)!

For if one does not do so who claims to be a child of God, then God asks, "how does the love of God abide in him?" In other words, how can such a person call himself a believer! So that is why God concludes here at 1 John 3:18, "Little children, let us not love with word or with tongue, but in deed and truth." In other words, let us, who profess to be believers, prove that we really are, and that the love of God is really in us by The Holy Spirit, by showing that love to those who are of the family of God in practical ways, such as helping to meet their needs, as that need becomes known to us, and in accordance with our means, since God is especially addressing Himself here to those of the family of God "whoever has the world's goods." What God wants to see from our lives as His children yet on earth is not just well-meaning words, but action to back up those words. While God's Son was on earth, He did not only give the word of God to those he met, but He met their physical needs as well.

God says that love through our actions is yet another sign of those who are true believers, and is part of what pleases Him

What an observant reader might have noticed so far is that in this first letter to believers through John, God is giving many signs that one can observe that will prove that one professing to be a child of God really is! And now at 1 John 3:19-22, God points out for us yet another such sign, noting what He there says, "[19] **We will know by this that we are of the truth, and will assure our heart before Him [20] in whatever our heart condemns us; for God is greater than our heart and knows all things. [21] Beloved, if our heart does not condemn us, we have confidence before God; [22] and whatever we ask we receive from Him, because we keep His commandments and do the things that are pleasing in His sight.**"

When God says in the first part of verse 3:19 here, "We will know by this that we are of the truth," He is making reference to what He has just said at 1 John 3:16-18 about God's kind of love being one that gives its all for others, same as God The Father gave His all when He gave His Son; and The Son of God gave all of Himself for the human race when He willingly died to pay the penalty due our sins. It was love that cost the giver something, and it was love in action, not just some pious words. And so we know we are of the truth, that is, truly children of God through salvation due to showing the same kind of love in action to those who are the same family of God as we are.

God also goes on and says that our love through our actions "will assure our hearts before Him." The word "assure" here is "Peitho" in the original, and speaks of gaining confidence. Therefore, those who love "in deed and truth" gain confidence in their hearts in their walk with God. As God goes on to say at 1 John 3:20, "in whatever our heart condemns us; for God is greater than our heart and knows all things." In other words, when we walk with God in the light of His word in ways that please Him, because they are part of His will for our lives; then we have a heart that is at rest in God's Presence, and not one that condemns, as when something is not quite right in our relationship with God. We may fool some people some of the time, but we can never fool God, for "God is greater than our hearts and knows all things," as also we read at Hebrews 4:13, "And there is no creature hidden from His sight, but all things are open and laid bare to the eyes of Him with whom we have to do."

At 1 John 3:21,22 here, God mentions a great benefit that believers all need to be aware of, which is a direct result of doing the things that are pleasing in His sight, such as loving others in deed and in truth, "[21] Beloved, if our heart does not condemn us, we have confidence before God; [22] and whatever we ask we receive from Him, because we keep His commandments and do the things that are pleasing in His sight." What God has in view here is prayer, which at its simplest is basically a child of God conversing with God The Father as one walks with Him in daily life. When we are in His will, because walking with Him in accordance with His word in the Bible, then we are pleasing in His sight and He delights to give us whatever we ask of Him.

Of course, we need to realize that being in God's will also means that we are living by His imparted life, that is, by His righteousness coming to us by The Holy Spirit in us, which further means that God is on control of our lives, so that what we request of Him is simply what He is leading us to request as part of His will for our lives! This is what God has in view for instance at Psalm 37:4, when He there tells His own, "Delight yourself in the Lord; and He will give you the desires of your heart." Serving God by serving others, especially those of the family of God, always has its benefits, noting what God further says to believers at Hebrews 6:10, "For God is not unjust so as to forget your work and the love which you have shown toward His name, in having ministered and in still ministering to the saints."

God has only one requirement for those who are His children yet on earth, which is that we simply live by faith in Him after salvation!

God now ends this third chapter of First John by introducing believers to a new truth at 1 John 3:23,24, to go along with the truth He has already made known, "[23] **This is His commandment, that we believe in the name of His Son Jesus Christ, and love one another, just as He commanded us. [24] The one who keeps His commandments abides in Him, and He in him. We know by this that He abides in us, by the Spirit whom He has given us**." The new truth that God is introducing here for the first time is, "that we believe in the name of His Son Jesus Christ." Let us note what God's

73

precious Son said at John 6:27-29 one day to those who were listening to him, "[27] Do not work for the food which perishes, but for the food which endures to eternal life, which the Son of Man will give to you, for on Him the Father, God, has set His seal." [28] Therefore they said to Him, "What shall we do, so that we may work the works of God?" [29] Jesus answered and said to them, "This is the work of God, that you believe in Him whom He has sent."

We need to notice that same truth of 1 John 3:23 at John 6:29 above, which is that we do "the works of God" when we "believe in Him whom He (God The Father) has sent." In other words, when we live by faith in God, by simply taking Him at His word by believing what He has told us in His word, we are doing the works of God! Let us notice here what God further says at Romans 1:16,17, "[16] For I am not ashamed of the gospel, for it is the power of God for salvation to everyone who believes, to the Jew first and also to the Greek. [17] For in it (that is, the gospel) the righteousness of God is revealed from faith to faith; as it is written, "But the righteous man shall live by faith." The critical truth to see here is that we are living by faith when we are walking by God's righteousness, that is, when we are living by God's imparted life coming to us automatically by The Holy Spirit in us as we walk with God with no known unconfessed sins in our lives!

Then when God goes on at 1 John 3:23 here and adds, "and love one another, just as He commanded us," we are to see that this will be the automatic result, namely loving those of the family of God, whenever we are living by faith, which as noted above, we do when we live by God's life imparted to us by The Holy Spirit as we walk with God with no known unconfessed sins in our lives. In other words, the love for other believers is the visible or observable sign that we are living by faith in God, and that we are living by God's imparted righteousness, and that we do indeed walk with God with no known unconfessed sins in our lives! As an evangelist knowing these truths, it does not take long for God's servant to determine where a person is spiritually whenever a person is encountered, no matter how encountered, for what a person says reveals what is in one's heart, noting what God says at Matthew 12:34b, "For the mouth speaks out of that which fills the heart." Such a determination is not meant to judge the person, but rather to simply know how best to minister to that person, in terms of whether one is a believer or an unbeliever.

God concludes here at 1 John 3:24 by saying that whoever "keeps His commandments," which is the expression of His will for believers, as made known in His word, such a one "abides in Him, and He in him." We have seen this word "abides" thirteen times already in First John, which is the Greek word "Meno," here meaning to remain or continue. Therefore, those believers who walk in obedience to God's word will find themselves walking with God and He with them, with God further disclosing here that one will be conscious of that walk with God "by the Spirit whom He has given us."

In other words, The Holy Spirit in us will grant us the fruit of the Spirit, as we see at Galatians 5:22,23, as experiential evidence that we are so walking with God, "[22] But the fruit of the Spirit is love, joy, peace, patience, kindness, goodness, faithfulness, [23] gentleness, self-control; against such things there is no law." Let us especially note the first three here for our present purpose, as what should be most recognizable in our experience, "love, joy, peace..." There have always been and always will be great blessings in God's children walking with God, with the most readily discernable personally being that supernatural love, joy, and peace of God filling our hearts!

CHAPTER FOUR

1 John 4:1-21

God teaches believers to beware of false prophets in the world

Twice so far in God's first letter through John He has warned believers about being deceived, first at John 2:26, when God said, "These things I have written to you concerning those who are trying to deceive you," and then the second time at 1 John 3;7 in part, "Little children, make sure no one deceives you..." This is pointed out here because one reason for God giving us all these signs of what characterizes truc believers is due to the fact that there are many impostors out in the world, who are out to deceive believers, because under they are under the influence of the devil, who is himself the deceiver, deceiving the whole world (Revelation 12:9).

And now, as we begin 1 John 4, we see God warning believers again about deceivers, when He says at verses 4:1-6 here, "**[1] Beloved, do not believe every spirit, but test the spirits to see whether they are from God, because many false prophets have gone out into the world. [2] By this you know the Spirit of God: every spirit that confesses that Jesus Christ has come in the flesh is from God; [3] and every spirit that does not confess Jesus is not from God; this is the spirit of the antichrist, of which you have heard that it is coming, and now it is already in the world. [4] You are from God, little children, and have overcome them; because greater is He who is in you than he who is in the world. [5] They are from the world; therefore they speak as from the world, and the world listens to them. [6] We are from God; he who knows God listens to us; he who is not from God does not**

listen to us. By this we know the spirit of truth and the spirit of error."

When God says to believers here to 'not believe every spirit" and to "test the spirits," He is talking about the human spirit of a person. In other words, the human spirit of a believer will be guided by The Holy Spirit, while the human spirit of an unbeliever will be guided by the devil, keeping in mind what God said at 1 John 3:10 in regards to the fact that one either belongs to God as His children (believers), or else one belongs to the devil as his children (unbelievers). And so that is why God goes on to say here at verse 4:1 that one is to "test the spirits," simply "to see if they are from God" or not. Then God gives a reason why a believer is to test the spirits, which is "because many false prophets have gone out into the world."

What is very important to keep in mind when God speaks about "prophets" here is that He is speaking of New Testament prophets, and not Old Testament prophets! The reason why this is the case is due to the fact that this is being said to believers in the third age of time, while all the occurrences of the word "prophet(s)" in the Old Testament have reference to the second age of time! That there are New Testament prophets is clear from passages such as the following, where they are mentioned, which are all in reference to the present third age of time (keeping in mind from Addendum A that the present third age started at Acts 2): Acts 11:27; 13:1; 15:32; 21:10; 1 Corinthians 12:28,29; 14:29,32,37; and Ephesians 3:5. All other references in the New Testament are to Old Testament prophets!

And what is also important to be aware of regarding prophets in the Old Testament is that these were men who were believers through whom God gave His word to other human beings. And so, false prophets were those who presumed to speak to others for God, noting for instance what God says at Jeremiah 14:14, "The prophets are prophesying falsehood in My name. I have neither sent them nor commanded them nor spoken to them; they are prophesying to you a false vision, divination, futility and the deception of their own minds." Claiming to speak for God when God had not raised one as a prophet was serious, noting what God says at Deuteronomy 18:20, "But the prophet who speaks a word presumptuously in My name which I have not commanded him to speak, or which he speaks in the name of other gods, that prophet shall die."

In the New Testament, God only raised prophets, who were believing men during the early stages of the present third age, until God's word making up the New Testament had been fully given to man by God. These prophets were replaced by shepherd/teachers in the local churches before the end of the first century AD, noting Ephesians 4:11, where we see apostles and prophets in place in the early stages of the present third age, then evangelists and shepherd/teachers replacing them after all the New Testament had been given by God and written down by believing men chosen by Him to do so. Let us note one example of New Testament prophets in action in a local gathering of believers on The Lord's day at 1 Corinthians 14:29-32, which was during the present third age before all the letters of the New Testament had been given by God, "[29] Let two or three prophets speak, and let the others pass judgment. [30] But if a revelation is made to another who is seated, the first one must keep silent. [31] For you can all prophesy one by one, so that all may learn and all may be exhorted; [32] and the spirits of prophets are subject to prophets." The reference to "a revelation" here meant the world of God being given to God's people through a New Testament prophet before that word had been permanently written down.

Coming back to 1 John 4, we note that God says at verse 4:1 that believers are to test the spirits because "many false prophets have gone out into the world (Kosmos)," that is, many are claiming to be speaking for God, when they are simply not of God, in terms of never having been raised of Him, or God ever speaking through them. The observant reader here will also have noticed that since we are almost at the end of the present third age, which means that 'prophets' have long been extinct from the churches, since the first century AD in fact, then anyone even claiming to be a prophet at this time anywhere in the world should be regarded as a "false prophet," simply because God no longer ever raises prophets to speak for Him, since His word has all been given that He had wanted to see contained in the New Testament!

At 1 John 4:2,3, God gives a test for believers to use for determining if one is speaking by The Holy Spirit, and therefore a believer, or whether one is simply speaking from one's spirit as an unbeliever, when God says there, "[2] By this you know the Spirit of God: every spirit that confesses that Jesus Christ has come in the flesh is from

God, [3] and every spirit that does not confess Jesus is not from God; this is the spirit of the antichrist, of which you have heard that it is coming, and now it is already in the world." And the reason that God gives this test is that only believers, as those who have The Holy Spirit indwelling in their human spirit, will be able to confess "that Jesus Christ has come in the flesh," simply because this is a truth that only The Holy Spirit can make known to a person. And so, unbelievers, in not having The Holy Spirit, because never having believed the gospel, will never confess or acknowledge as a reality "that Jesus Christ has come in the flesh."

In fact, God says here that every person "that does not confess Jesus" is not only "not from God," but God says such people have "the spirit of the antichrist." We have already been introduced to a person known as "the antichrist" at John 2:18, who is coming on the world scene immediately after the present third age of time ends, and who will rule the whole world of unbelievers, being himself under the direct authority of the devil (Revelation 13:1-8). What is important to realize here is that all unbelievers have "the spirit of the antichrist," which is why God says here that "it is already in the world," and which is also why all unbelievers on earth, bar none, will freely serve the antichrist in the coming last seven years of the second age of time, which for those coming to personally know God during that period of time it will be a time of tribulation (Matthew 24:9,21).

God then seeks to encourage believers, so that none will fear the presence of unbelievers in the world, when God goes on to say at 1 John 4:4, "You are from God, little children, and have overcome them; because greater is He who is in you than he who is in the world." The "them" here is a reference to unbelievers in this present world, while "he who is in the world" is a reference to Satan, the devil. Therefore, believers can be encouraged to know that we are not only "from God" as also His children yet on earth, but we also have God indwelling us through His Son by The Holy Spirit in our spirit, Who is much greater that the devil who is in the world directing the unbelievers out there. And the full import of what God is saying here will really hit home when we remember that God is eternally existing with all power over all creation, being Sovereign and in total control at all times of all that exists; while the devil is a fallen angel and unbelievers are fallen human beings, all part of God's original creation, so that nothing can ever be greater than God our Father!

Then at 1 John 4:5,6, God closes this section by giving a contrast of what characterizes believers in comparison to unbelievers, so that believers will not be deceived when encountering human beings such as these in the world, "[5] They (unbelievers) are from the world (Kosmos); therefore they speak as from the world (Kosmos), and the world (Kosmos) listens to them. [6] We (believers) are from God; he who knows God listens to us; he who is not from God does not listen to us. By this we know the spirit of truth and the spirit of error." Let us recall here for a moment what God had said at 1 John 2:15,16 in part, regarding "the world (Kosmos)" here in view, [15] Do not love the world nor the things in the world. If anyone loves the world, the love of the Father is not in him. [16] For all that is in the world... is not from the Father, but is from the world," which world is at the present time under the devil's control (1 John 5:19).

Therefore, since unbelievers "are from the world," then it is only to be expected that the world listens to them, in terms of unbelievers understanding each other very well, because they speak the same language, so to speak. On the other hand, it is only to be expected that believers, who "are from God" will listen to other believers who also know God, all being part of the same family. Unbelievers will not listen to believers, simply because they do not know God. That is why there is no point ever trying to argue with an unbeliever, not because we can never win that argument, but simply because they have the "spirit of the antichrist" and therefore "the spirit of error," so that they cannot ever comprehend the truth, since that truth is from God and requires The Holy Spirit in salvation to make it known to one's spirit, which they do not have, not knowing God in salvation themselves. And so this is yet another test that God gives here to recognize unbelievers, because they are those who will not listen to believers, being children of the devil, and like him, having "the spirit of error."

God again returns to the test of love to help believers discern those persons who are of God and from those who are not

At 1 John 4:7,8 here, God again returns to talk to believers about the test of love, as it is what distinguishes a believer from an unbeliever, letting us know 'why' in what He now says, "[7] **Beloved, let us love one another, for love is from God; and everyone who loves is born of God and knows God. [8] The one who does not love**

does not know God, for God is love." God discloses quite a truth here when He says that "love is from God," and therefore "everyone who loves is born of God and knows God." In other words, as we have seen already from Romans 5:5, namely that God's love was poured into our hearts by The Holy Spirit coming to indwell our spirits at the moment of our salvation. This was the moment that we were born spiritually into God's family.

And that is why God says here, "Beloved, let us love one another," not only because we are part of the same family of God as believers, but because love is the one characteristic above all the others (Galatians 5:22) that distinguishes the children of God from those who are not, for as God continues here He says that "the one who does not love does not know God," for to know God is to love as evidence of being part of the family of God. To know God is to love, since "God is love." That is why God's Son said to His followers at John 13:35, "By this all men will know that you are My disciples, if you have love for one another." In other words, love for one another will identify you as believers before a watching world.

God has already demonstrated by example what the love He wants believers to display is like

At 1 John 4:9-11 here, God gives believers an example of the love that He has already displayed to the human race, and which He wants believers to display, when He now goes on and says, "[9] **By this the love of God was manifested in us** (that is, toward us, or among us), **that God has sent His only begotten Son into the world so that we might live through Him. [10] In this is love, not that we loved God, but that He loved us and sent His Son to be the propitiation for our sins. [11] Beloved, if God so loved us, we also ought to love one another**." The word "manifested" at verse 4:9 here is "Phaneroo" in the original and refers to what is revealed in its true character. In other words, God showed the true character of His love for mankind steeped in sin when He "sent His only begotten Son into the world (Kosmos)" of lost sinners… "to be the propitiation for our sins." We have already encountered this world "propitiation" at 1 John 2:2, where we saw that it is "Hilasmos" in the original, and speaks of the fact that God's Son is in Himself the sacrifice offered to God The Father in His death at the cross as payment for sins; not only as we saw there, for the sins of believers, but also in payment

82

for the sins of the whole world, even of those who do not believe in God.

What God wants believers to grasp here is that when God gave His Son to come to this earth and take on a human body in our likeness - but minus our sinful nature, being born of a virgin in the innocence of Adam - that was the fullest extent of God's love, in that was all the love that God had to give, which is why we read at John 3:16 in part, "For God so loved the world, that He gave His only begotten Son..." And in a similar manner, when God's Son willingly came to be the sacrifice in Himself in death at the cross in payment for the sins of mankind, it was the fullest extent of the love of God that He could display in that He gave His all in dying in the place of sinners, which is why we read of that love that He displayed in this way at 1 John 3:16 in part, "We know love by this, that He laid down His life for us..." In other words, in giving His life for us, God's Son, The Lord Jesus Christ, was giving a full demonstration of the love of God in that He gave all He could give, which was all of Himself! So that is why God concludes here at 1 John 4:11 and says to believers, "Beloved, if God so loved us, we also ought to love one another."

Back at 1 John 3:18, God had said to believers, "Little children, let us not love with word or with tongue, but in deed and truth." And that is now what God is calling those who are His own on earth to do, to love as He Himself has ever loved. Since we cannot love by the same example of God's Son in giving all of Himself for a sinful human race, since this is unique to God, nevertheless He does call those who regard themselves as believers "to love one another," that is, to at the least love those who are of the family of God! And if we are to love as He loved, then we will willingly be giving all of ourselves for one another as brothers and sisters in Christ!

One may be reading this at this point and be wondering, 'how do I do that, in terms of giving all of myself for my brothers and sisters in Christ'? And the answer here can be found in a statement at 1 John 4:9 that we have not yet commented on, where God says, "...God has sent His only begotten Son into the world so that we might live through Him." What God means by "live through Him" here, that is, through His Son, is that God's Son died in the place of the sinner, not only that one might have the forgiveness of sins in believing in Him, but that one might also have eternal life! And as was mentioned numerous times already, the moment that we believe the gospel of God regarding His Son, God gives us His Holy Spirit to indwell our human spirit. And in The Holy Spirit coming to indwell a believer at salvation, God's life is also imparted for one to now live by, instead of living by one's sinful nature, as before salvation. This life of God is eternal life, being God's own righteous life or righteousness. So as we continue with God with no known unconfessed sins in our lives after salvation, God continues to impart His life through His Son by His Spirit in us for us to live by as believers. And as we live by that life, then we can be sure that we are living by God's love also, for His love cannot be separated from His life. Therefore, that is how we live through God's Son, The Lord Jesus Christ, after salvation, and how we can love as God loves in terms of giving our all, since we deny all of self in now serving God in this way!

We are also to see and remember that the love of God is a love that originated with God, even before we yet knew Him. God is The One Who sought us out and drew us to Himself for salvation (John 6:37,44,65), which is why God says in the first part of 1 John 4:10, "In this is love, not that we loved God, but that He loved us..." All originates with God, which is why God tells believers at 1 Corinthians 8:6, "yet for us there is but one God, the Father, from whom are all things and we exist for Him; and one Lord, Jesus Christ, by whom are all things, and we exist through Him," in that the life of God is always imparted through Him to us by The Holy Spirit in our spirit.

When believers love another, love is perfected in them

God makes yet another truth known to believers when He says at 1 John 4:12,13, "[12] **No one has seen God at any time; if we love one another, God abides in us, and His love is perfected in us. [13] By this we know that we abide in Him and He in us, because He has given us of His Spirit.**" And before knowing what that truth is, we first need to know what is meant by the word "perfected." It is "Teleioo" in the original Greek and means to bring to an intended end so as to complete. So what God wants to bring to an intended end so as to complete it, or perfect it, is as we see at verse 4:12 here, "His love... in us." And the obvious question here is: How is that accomplished?

Well, in the first part of the verse, we are told, "No one has ever seen God at any time; if we love one another, God abides in us, and His

84

love is perfected in us." By now, we should all be aware that when we love one another as believers, then it is because we are living by God's Spirit, also meaning that we are walking with God and living by His imparted life, with no known unconfessed sins in our lives. This then means that "God abides in us," in the sense of continuing to live in us and through us to accomplish His will, in us and in the world. And for our present purpose here, it also means that "His love is perfected in us," in the sense that we are now being conformed to the image of His Son, The Lord Jesus Christ!

We can never see God The Father, but one reason God gave His Son was so that mankind might have a visual representation of God in looking at God's Son, noting what The Lord Jesus Christ said at John 14:9 to one of His followers one day, "Jesus said to him, "Have I been so long with you, and yet you have not come to know Me, Philip? He who has seen Me has seen the Father; how can you say, 'Show us the Father'?" " Let us also note what God says of His Son in this regard at Colossians 1:15 in part, "He is the image of the invisible God..." Yet, while this is true, God nevertheless never allowed a physical image of His Son to be made, nor did He ever give any physical description of Him! Why? Because God wanted the image of God as portrayed in His Son while on earth to later be reproduced in us as believers as we live by God's life, and therefore love as He loves, for then that image is being perfected in us, which is what God intended all along!

Let us look at an example here to help us understand this in another context. This is taken from what John the Baptist was led of God to say at John 3:27-30, after some Jews came to him and told him that people were flocking to Jesus, where before He came, they had been flocking to him, "[27] John answered and said, "A man can receive nothing unless it has been given him from heaven. [28] You yourselves are my witnesses that I said, 'I am not the Christ,' but, 'I have been sent ahead of Him.' [29] He who has the bride is the bridegroom; but the friend of the bridegroom, who stands and hears him, rejoices greatly because of the bridegroom's voice. So this joy of mine has been made full. [30] He must increase, but I must decrease." "

When John the Baptist said here that "He must increase, but I must decrease," he primarily meant the ministry of God's Son on earth was to increase while his own ministry must decrease and eventually come to an end. However, spiritually speaking this is also true in regard to what we personally as believers are becoming, in terms of being conformed to the image of God's Son, so that we are day by day becoming more and more like His Son while He was on earth in God His Father's service. In other words, and this is very important to grasp here is that as we begin our new life with God at salvation, it is in a sense 'all of self,' in that we are full of ourselves as yet and do not realize it. However, little by little and day by day, as we live by God's imparted life and not by our sinful nature, then spiritually speaking we are in fact 'decreasing' while He, God's Son in us by The Holy Spirit, is 'increasing.' And looked at in the context of 1 John 4:12 now, in terms of God's love being perfected in us, we are to see that as we become conformed to the image of God's Son, then God's love is reaching its intended end in us, which is to have us love others as God's Son Himself loved others while on earth!

Then God concludes here at 1 John 4:13 with the truth we have already been introduced to at 1 John 3:24, namely that "by this we know that we abide in Him and He in us, because He has given us of His Spirit." In other words, God's Spirit in our spirit gives us experiential evidence to our hearts and minds that we are walking with God and He with us through "the fruit of The Spirit" (Galatians 5:22,23) being supernaturally produced in and through our lives, with the most prominent being the love, joy, and peace of God flooding our lives and overflowing to others. God says in regards to His Son while on earth at John 3:34, "For He whom God has sent speaks the words of God; for He gives the Spirit without measure." In other words, there was no sinful nature in God's Son to limit the extent of the working of God's Spirit in Him, in that He worked to the fullest extent possible.

And so, as a believer continues to live by God's life, with no known unconfessed sins in one's life; one becomes more and more conformed to the image of God's Son. We are personally aware of it due to the spiritual sense of wellbeing we have, in terms of the love, joy, and peace of God flooding our hearts and minds; however, in order to ensure that we do not get all swell-headed with pride here, we remain unaware of the spiritual effect that we are having upon others we come in contact with, both believers and unbelievers. We do know that there is such an effect due to what God says to believers in this regard at 2 Corinthians 2:14-16, "[14] But thanks be to God, who always leads us in triumph in Christ, and manifests through us the sweet aroma of the knowledge of Him in every place. [15] For we are a fragrance of Christ to God among those who are being saved and among those who are perishing; [16] to the one an aroma from death to death, to the other an aroma from life to life. And who is adequate for these things?"

God gives believers yet another test for discerning those who are believers

Then at 1 John 4:14,15, God gives believers yet another test to help one discern who is a believer, when He goes on to say, "[14] **We have seen and testify that the Father has sent the Son to be the Savior of the world. [15] Whoever confesses that Jesus is the Son of God, God abides in him, and he in God.**" The reason that God begins and says what He does at verse 4:14 here is that it directly impacts what is then said at verse 4:15! And so, at verse 4:14, we have the apostle John's own testimony, as one who personally walked with God's Son, The Lord Jesus Christ, during the three and half years of His public ministry. Therefore, that is why he can be a witness along with the other apostles and say here, "We have seen and testify" to the fact "that the Father has sent The Son to be the Savior of the world."

Even prior to being chosen by God to write these three short letters of First, Second, and Third John, the apostle John had been chosen of God to write what is known as 'The gospel according to John,' which had the stated aim, as we read at John 20:31, adding verse 30 for context, "[30] Therefore many other signs Jesus also performed in the presence of the disciples, which are not written in this book; [31] but these have been written so that you may believe that Jesus is the Christ, the Son of God; and that believing you may have life in His name." We have already looked extensively at the meaning of that statement "Jesus is the Christ" when looking at 1 John 2:22, and there pointed out that to say that one believes that "Jesus is the Christ" is to believe that God's eternally existing Son, Who had the name "Christ" before He took on our humanity, was then given the name "Jesus" at His physical birth into this world, which meant that one believed that God had sent His Son into the world, which was for the purpose of saving some of the human race for God (noting

87

Matthew 1:21). This is now what John is led of God to give testimony to at 1 John 4:14, when he says, "We have seen and testify that the Father has sent the Son to be the Savior of the world."

Therefore, to confess, as we see at 1 John 4:15, that "Jesus is the Son of God," is to believe that Jesus is the Christ, that is, that He came to earth and took on human flesh, minus our sinful nature, in being born of a virgin in the innocence of Adam, since "Jesus" is the proper Name of God's Son now in human flesh! And so, whoever confesses this must be a believer, which also means that "God abides in him, and he in God." In other words, God is present in the life, which renders one a true child of God. Therefore, no unbelievers will ever confess that "Jesus is the Son of God," simply because God is not present by His Holy Spirit in that person's life, for as was stated already, it is The Holy Spirit in the life of a person who discloses to one's heart and mind that Jesus is the Christ, and therefore, The Son of God! Let us note what God says at 1 Corinthians 2:14 here, "But a natural man (that is, an unbeliever without The Holy Spirit) does not accept the things of the Spirit of God, for they are foolishness to him; and he cannot understand them, because they are spiritually appraised."

God's love indwelling believers casts out all fear of judgment

We then see God introduce yet another truth at 1 John 4:16-18 that He had not yet mentioned, but which can now be mentioned due having been introduced to the truth of God's love. And so we there read, "**[16] We have come to know and have believed the love which God has for us. God is love, and the one who abides in love abides in God, and God abides in him. [17] By this, love is perfected with us, so that we may have confidence in the day of judgment; because as He is, so also are we in this world. [18] There is no fear in love; but perfect love casts out fear, because fear involves punishment, and the one who fears is not perfected in love.**"

If one is a believer, then one has "come to know" by experiential evidence in one's heart and mind, and therefore has "believed the love which God has for" believers, since "God is love," as being the chief characteristic of His Being, as what a believer therefore first experiences when The Holy Spirit first comes to indwell our hearts and fills us with the love of God at the moment of salvation (noting

88

again Romans 5:5). The believer who continues to live by God's love after salvation, by living by God's life – which one does when one lives with no known unconfessed sins in one's life – then that believer continues to walk with God while God continues His work in the believer.

We need to see here that God's indwelling through His Son by The Holy Spirit in a believer is never without effect. In other words, it is always for the purpose of accomplishing His will through that believer, noting what God tells us at Philippians 2:13, "for it is God who is at work in you, both to will and to work for His good pleasure." God is not in us to sit on the fence and watch us perform for Him! He is in us to do all that He saved us to do through us as His own workmanship, noting what He tells us at Ephesians 2:10, "For we are His workmanship, created in Christ Jesus (at the moment of one's salvation) for good works, which God prepared beforehand so that we would walk in them." Those "good works" here is what God is in us to accomplish after we become a child of His after salvation.

Let us note what the apostle Paul said at Romans 15:18 in part regarding his ministry as an apostle, "For I will not presume to speak of anything except what Christ has accomplished through me..." And this was not an isolated case, as we note at Acts 21:19 what the apostle Paul there said to the elders of the local church at Jerusalem, "After he had greeted them, he began to relate one by one the things which God had done among the Gentiles through his ministry." We are to realize that this is so for believers on earth because it was so for God's Son, The Lord Jesus Christ, while He was on earth at His first coming from Heaven to earth, since He was a Pattern for the life that pleases God, noting what we read at 2 Corinthians 5:19 in part in this regard, "namely, that God was in Christ reconciling the world to Himself..." And so, that is why God says to believers at 1 Corinthians 1:31 in part, "Let him who boasts, boast in the Lord."

Coming back to 1 John 4, God then continues at verse 4:17 and says, "by this...," in reference to what has just been stated at verse 4:16 being true of us as believers; then this is the result, in that "love is perfected with us," which, as we have seen, simply means that God is bringing love to its intended end, which is to conform us to the image of God's Son, The Lord Jesus Christ, so that when He comes, we may be as God says at Philippians 1:6, "For I am confident of this very thing, that He who began a good work in you will perfect it until the day of Christ Jesus," and also at 1 Thessalonians 5:23, "Now may the God of peace Himself sanctify you (that is, set you apart for His will) entirely; and may your spirit and soul and body be preserved complete, without blame at the coming of our Lord Jesus Christ."

God then continues at 1 John 4:17 and now introduces the new truth He has here in mind, when He goes on to say, that if what has been said is true of us, in terms of love being perfected with us as believers, then this is also true in us, in that "we may have confidence in the day of judgment; because as He is, so are we in this world." The "day of judgment" that God has in view here is the last judgment of time, after the fourth age of time, that we see God mention at Revelation 20:11-15, which is when the unbelievers of the four ages of time are all raised from the dead at the same time, for all will have died physically (Hebrews 9:27), and now stand before God to be judged on this one thing, as to whether they believed the gospel regarding God's Son during one's stay on earth or not. And since none will have had their names written in God's book of life, where He writes one's name as one becomes a believer, then all of these will be cast from God's Presence forever into the lake of fire, which is eternal hell. Let us note what God says at Hebrews 10:31, "It is a terrifying thing to fall into the hands of the living God."

However, for believers, because we have believed and are God's children being conformed to the image of God's Son, so that we are like Him on earth, then we have nothing to fear regarding this final judgment of time, since God's Son bore at the cross God's judgment against sin on behalf of the human race! Praise be to God for that! One of my favorites hymns of the faith is 'What Love It Was,' and the first stanza goes as follows: 'What love it was that brought Thee down, down to the depths in which I lay, that made Thee leave Thy glory throne to thread Thy way in Servant's form, to death to go that I might never judgment know.' How true, and how blessed we are!

That is why God can say at 1 John 4:18, "There is no fear in love; but perfect love casts out fear, because fear involves punishment, and the one who fears is not perfected in love." When we are walking with God by His righteous life, with no known unconfessed sins in our lives, we are walking by the "perfect love" that "casts out fear." Since we have no known unconfessed sins in our lives, then we are not under Gods judgment due to sin, but rather are basking in the love, joy, and peace of God, where there is no fear! As God says to believers at Romans 8:1, who are so walking with Him, "Therefore there is now no condemnation for those who are in Christ Jesus."

When God says here, "the one who fears is not perfected in love," we are to see that this now refers to unbelievers, since they are certainly not being "perfected in love." We also know that this refers to unbelievers due to the fact that only believers are those who fear, because as we have seen, "fear involves punishment," and that at "the day of judgment," which is the final judgment of time, which relates only to all the unbelievers of the four ages of time. As God says at Hebrews 10:29, which is true of every unbeliever to ever live on earth, "How much severer punishment do you think he will deserve who has trampled under foot the Son of God, and has regarded as unclean the blood of the covenant by which he was sanctified, and has insulted the Spirit of grace?" There is a consequence for rejecting God, which unbelievers of time will discover at the final judgment. Until then, unbelievers can only fear, as God says of them at Isaiah 48:22, "There is no peace for the wicked," says the Lord." "

God gives yet another test to discern believers from unbelievers as relating to the love of God

God has ways to flush out those who claim to be believers and are not, with our now seeing yet another test that God gives believers to discern those who are His from those who are not, in what He now says at 1 John 4:19-21, "[19] **We love, because He first loved us. [20] If someone says, "I love God," and hates his brother, he is a liar; for the one who does not love his brother whom he has seen, cannot love God whom he has not seen. [21] And this commandment we have from Him, that the one who loves God should love his brother also.**" The test that God gives at verse 4:20 here relates to the love of God at verse 4:19, in that "He first loved us" in salvation, as wholly a work of God's grace and power alone, as something we did not deserve. And so we know love and therefore love, when we walk by God's life, with no known unconfessed sins in our lives. With salvation came God's love, so that we can love others with His supernatural love (Romans 5:5).

What this means then, when we come to the test at verse 4:20 here, that God gives believers to discern those who are unbelievers, is if God's love is not present, due to one having never believed in God and so never having experienced salvation so as to have received God's supernatural love to love others, is that one will "not love his brother" – which is one's fellow man here – even if one might say, "I love God." 'For if the supernatural love of God is not present in the life in order to love a fellow human being that one can see,' says God here, 'then how can one love God whom one has not seen?' The fact that one does not love "his brother whom he has seen," means that one "hates his brother" and is therefore a clear indication that one does not love God, and therefore, "he is a liar," being yet an unbeliever! We are also to see here that this is not a new subject, as it was first raised by God back at 1 John 2:9-11.

As we see at 1 John 4:21, loving our fellow man is not an option for believers, since we are on earth to now be His Hands, Feet, and Mouth, representing Him on earth, same as His Son did while here at His first coming as a Pattern for us. Let us think on this for a moment. When God's Son was on earth in human flesh, God had one Person through Whom He worked and taught, which was mainly in Israel. Now, with God's Son being back in Heaven at The Father's right Hand, and with The Holy Spirit now having come to indwell believers in all countries on earth, that means God now has many more persons on earth that He can speak and work through - and for what relates to our present subject - to love through!

Therefore, when God says here at verse 4:21 "that the one who loves God should love his brother also," and then gives that as a commandment, He is indicating that we have a responsibility as believers yet on earth, which is to live as His Son lived, which is sin-free. God's Son was sinless to start with, that is true, however, we can walk with no known unconfessed sins in our lives, and as we do, then we are being imparted God's life to live by, which means we have God's love in us to love others as He Himself loves us. And so, true believers will live with no known unconfessed sins, thereby showing love for God, and at the same time being enabled to love one's fellow man, as God Himself would if He were still in His Son on earth! We will see God return to the same theme in the first three verses of the next chapter.

CHAPTER FIVE

1 John 5:1-21

A consolidation by God of truth already made known to believers

As was already mentioned earlier in the book, chapter and verse divisions are not part of the original text in the Greek as given to mankind by God, but rather were inserted by men at some point in history. To God, this letter is but one continuing whole from start to finish. And so, as we begin 1 John 5, we note that verses 5:1-3 are a consolidation of truth He has already shared, and had especially been dealing with as we ended 1 John 4. And so, we note that at 1 John 5:1-3, God goes on to say here, "[1] **Whoever believes that Jesus is the Christ is born of God, and whoever loves the Father loves the child born of Him. [2] By this we know that we love the children of God, when we love God and observe His commandments. [3] For this is the love of God, that we keep His commandments; and His commandments are not burdensome.**"

One has probably also noticed in reading God's letter of 1 John so far as part of this book that God often arrives at the same truth a number of times, but often coming from different angles. And what has just been said is especially true in regards to the many tests that God has given believers in this particular letter to help one discern who the children of God really are in the world, where the great majority are unbelievers. So it should not surprise us to hear God say at verse 5:1 here, "Whoever believes that Jesus is the Christ is born of God," which further means, without God having to spell that out for us by now, that 'whoever does not believe that Jesus is The Christ is not born of God, and therefore not a believer.' And here, God clearly states the truth already brought out that one needs to be born of God in order to know for sure that "Jesus is the Christ," that is, that The Person born in human flesh as 'Jesus' is His eternally-existing Son, Christ, Who has come from Heaven to earth to take on the sinless body prepared for Him in the womb of the virgin (Hebrews 10:5).

In a similar way, God goes on in the rest of 1 John 5:1 and says that "whoever loves the Father loves the child born of Him," which is another way of coming at the truth already brought out at 1 John 4:20,21, that if one has the love of God, from the moment of salvation onward, which comes to us by The Holy Spirit as He comes to indwell our spirit at our moment of believing, then one will not only love one's fellowman, but also other believers as part of the family of God, which one sees, and also God, whom one does not see. However, this will of course not be true for one who is an unbeliever, who will not even know The Father, let alone love Him, and so will certainly not love ones fellowman, and even less believers. What this means then is that one needs to be a believer, so as to have The Holy Spirit, in order to be able to love God The Father and other believers, which is "the child born of Him" here.

What also needs to be noticed here is that God does not say 'whoever loves The Son,' but rather "whoever loves The Father," which is an impossibility without first loving The Son of God, Who came to this world in order to make God The Father known! Let us note what God tells us at Matthew 11:27, through His Son Who at the point of saying this was walking the earth among men, "All things have been handed over to Me by My Father; and no one knows the Son except the Father; nor does anyone know the Father except the Son, and anyone to whom the Son wills to reveal Him." What this means is that one first needs to believe The Son for salvation in order to receive The Holy Spirit to make known to us The Son, Christ, as now being Jesus in human flesh, Who in turn makes The Father known to a believer!

And again, one of the reasons for God giving us His truth in such ways is that it is only by The Holy Spirit that this can be understood by believers, which again means unbelievers would not be able to understand this, noting what God says in this regard at 1 Corinthians 2:12,14, "[12] Now we have received, not the spirit of the world, but the Spirit who is from God, so that we may know the things freely given to us by God... [14] But a natural man does not accept the things of the Spirit of God, for they are foolishness to him; and he cannot understand them, because they are spiritually appraised." In this way, God gives us all that is necessary to walk with Him in the truth, free from error, and free from the trickery of men!

When God goes on to say at 1 John 5:2, "By this we know that we love the children of God, when we love God and observe His commandments," He is again consolidating truth already stated, although expressed in different worlds. For what needs to be observed here is that obedience is always a sign that one is a child of God through salvation, as was already pointed out, and the further truth to be grasped here is that we are automatically obeying God's commandments when we are living by God's life imparted to us by The Holy Spirit in us, as we walk with God with no known unconfessed sins in our lives! These are important truths to ever keep in mind. And as God says here at verse 5:2, if we are obeying God's commandments, this means we are walking with Him and doing His will, and we are indeed loving God and the children born of God, like us, as believers.

In God then saying at 1 John 5:3, "For this is the love of God, that we keep His commandments..." He is indicating to believers that to obey His commandments is a good primary demonstration of our love for God, since we are in this way carrying out His will as we live here on earth as His children. Let us note here what God's Son said to His followers at John 14;15, "If you love Me, you will keep My commandments." And what needs to be remembered here is that when God's Son was on earth, He stated at John 6:38, "For I have come down from heaven, not to do My own will, but the will of Him who sent Me." Since doing the will of God is what one does when one obeys His commandments, then that is what God's Son was doing during His whole time on earth, obeying His Father's commands, and therefore doing His will. And so, as believers we are walking as God's precious Son walked, loving God The Father as He did, when we are obeying God's commands, noting the truth we have been introduced to back at 1 John 2:6, where God said, "the one who says he abides in Him (that is, His Son) ought himself to walk in the same manner as He walked."

Then God concludes at verse 5:3 by letting believers know that "His commandments are not burdensome." This is true, since we must remember that as we walk with God with no known unconfessed sins in our lives we are being imparted God's own life by The Holy Spirit to live by. As we have seen, to so walk with God is a life of love, peace and joy, where we have His strength and power to carry on, which we can be sure is no burden! And let us also recall that as we live by God's righteous life, or righteousness, moment by moment, then we are obeying all His commandments, as we are carrying out His will on earth in the same manner as His own Son, The Lord Jesus Christ, Himself did while He was on earth, and we can be sure that His life with His Father was not burdensome! And let us also note what God's Son promises at Matthew 11:28-30, in inviting people to come to Him for salvation, "[28] Come to Me, all who are weary and heavy-laden, and I will give you rest. [29] Take My yoke upon you and learn from Me, for I am gentle and humble in heart, and you will find rest for your souls. [30] For My yoke is easy and My burden is light." We can take God at His word on that!

If one is a true believer, one is automatically an overcomer while here on earth!

God then goes on to introduce us to a new truth at 1 John 5:4,5, about those who are overcomers in this world, when He says, "[4] **For whatever is born of God overcomes the world; and this is the victory that has overcome the world — our faith. [5] Who is the one who overcomes the world, but he who believes that Jesus is the Son of God?**" We note that God defines for us who is an overcomer in His sight in this present world, looking at this from three different perspectives or angles, the first two being at verse 5:4 and the third at verse 5:5. And so, at verse 5:4, God gives the first answer as to who "overcomes the world," which is everyone who "is born of God." And since all believers are those born of God, that is, of having experienced a spiritual birth by The Holy Spirit at the moment of one's salvation, which is at the moment of having believed in His Son, this then means that all believers will overcome the world! The translators from the original Greek into English use the word "whatever" here, which is "Pas" in the original, which has the primary meaning of 'all,' that is, of constituting the totality of the persons referred to, without leaving any out.

Then in the last part of 1 John 5:4, God says, "this is the victory that has overcome the world – our faith." The word "victory" here is "Nike" in the original, which occurs only here in God's word and points us to "our faith," as what assures our being overcomers in the world. In other words, our faith in God, which is our believing the gospel leading to our salvation, is God-given (2 Peter 1:1), as a gift from Him (Ephesians 2:8), so that we are assured of being overcomers in this world as now a child of God, as wholly a work of God's grace and power, and this is something that is true for every child of God!

Then the third definition that God gives of "the one who overcomes the world" is at 1 John 5:5, when He says that it is "he who believes that Jesus Christ is The Son of God." Again, this is true only of believers, and that of every believer, which means that all believers are therefore overcomers in this world! As to the words "overcome" and "overcomes," which God uses three times here in these two verses, we are to note that these are the word "Nikao" in the original, which also has the meaning of being 'conquerors.'

And let us note that God does not say here, as He did before, anything about believing that 'Jesus is the Christ,' but rather here says, "that Jesus Christ is the Son of God." In other words, one believes that Jesus Christ is God's Son in human flesh, which now has no connection to before the Incarnation! Please note the distinction here. To believe the statement "Jesus is the Christ," means one believes that God's eternally existing Son, Christ, took on the body prepared for Him in the womb of the virgin to be born into this world in human flesh as "Jesus." It involves God's Son before the Incarnation, going through the Incarnation, and after the Incarnation. However, to believe "that Jesus is the Son of God" involves only after the Incarnation. And so, this is another test here that God gives, since no unbeliever will believe this from one's heart and mind, since only The Holy Spirit indwelling one's heart can make that a truth to be believed, and only believers have The precious Holy Spirit.

The testimony of The Spirit, the water, and the blood

Having introduced God's Son, Jesus Christ, as being Whom believers believe in, not only for salvation, but also for being overcomers in this world through Him, God now goes on at 1 John 5:6-8 and introduces us to the testimony that The Holy Spirit, the water, and the blood, give of Him, there reading, "[6] **This is the One**

who came by water and blood, Jesus Christ; not with (literally 'in') **the water only, but with** (literally 'in') **the water and with** (literally 'in') **the blood. It is the Spirit who testifies, because the Spirit is the truth.** [7] **For there are three that testify:** [8] **the Spirit and the water and the blood; and the three are in agreement.**" And what most reading this will attest to is that this is likely the most difficult portion of God's First letter given through John for us to understand. We need the mind of God, as given by The Holy Spirit, in order to correctly understand what God is saying here.

And the obvious question which confronts us here, since we know that "the Spirit" is a reference to The Holy Spirit, is what does "the water" and "the blood" refer to? To begin with, the word "water" is "Hudor" in the original, while the word "blood" is "Haima" in the original Greek, which words are to be taken as literal in meaning. What is also critical to keep in mind here is that the witness of The Spirit, the water, and the blood relate to God's Son, Jesus Christ, after His Incarnation. In other words, this witness here relates to after God's Son had been born of a virgin and was found in appearance on earth as a Man. And so what is critical to grasp here is that the witness relates to the start and the end of the ministry of God's Son, Jesus Christ, on earth. What this means then is that the "water" here is the water of His baptism by John the Baptist at the start of His ministry on earth, while the "blood" is a reference to His blood shed unto death at the cross on behalf of the human race, to pay the penalty due its sins, which sacrifice ended His public ministry on earth!

First then, let us note what we God tells us at Mark 1:9-11, "[9] In those days Jesus came from Nazareth in Galilee and was baptized by John in the Jordan. [10] Immediately coming up out of the water (Hudor), He saw the heavens opening, and the Spirit like a dove descending upon Him; [11] and a voice came out of the heavens: "You are My beloved Son, in You I am well-pleased." Here we see that as God's Son, Jesus Christ, started His public ministry on earth at the age of thirty (Luke 3:23), by being baptized by John the Baptist in the waters of the Jordan River, The Holy Spirit descended like a dove and rested upon Him, while The Father declared from Heaven that this Jesus Christ now in human flesh on earth was indeed His Son!

What is also very important to grasp here is that God's Son, Jesus Christ, was here identifying with lost sinners in being baptized in water by John the Baptist, noting what God says about John's baptism at Mark 1:4,5, "[4] John the Baptist appeared in the wilderness preaching a baptism of repentance for the forgiveness of sins. [5] And all the country of Judea was going out to him, and all the people of Jerusalem; and they were being baptized by him in the Jordan River, confessing their sins." Since Jesus Christ was indeed God's Son now in human flesh, then this meant that He was sinless and had no need of water baptism. However, in order to identify with a human race lost in sin, and since He had come to take away the sin of the world, then He also underwent the water of baptism to start His public ministry, noting here very carefully what God led John the Baptist to say at John 1:29-34, "[29] The next day he (John the Baptist) saw Jesus coming to him and said, "Behold, the Lamb of God who takes away the sin of the world! [30] This is He on behalf of whom I said, 'After me comes a Man who has a higher rank than I, for He existed before me.' [31] I did not recognize Him, but so that He might be manifested to Israel, I came baptizing in water." [32] John testified saying, "I have seen the Spirit descending as a dove out of heaven, and He remained upon Him. [33] I did not recognize Him, but He who sent me to baptize in water said to me, 'He upon whom you see the Spirit descending and remaining upon Him, this is the One who baptizes in the Holy Spirit.' [34] I myself have seen, and have testified that this is the Son of God."

And as already noted, the "blood" is a reference to the end of the public ministry of God's Son, Jesus Christ, at the cross, where He gave His lifeblood for the sins of the human race. Having started His public ministry by identifying with a sinful human race in the water's of the baptism of John the Baptist, He now concludes His public ministry in shedding His blood at the cross to pay the penalty of death due the sins of the human race. Let us note what God makes known to us about the blood shed at the cross of His Son, Jesus Christ, at Hebrews 9:11-14, "[11] But when Christ appeared as a high priest of the good things to come, He entered through the greater and more perfect tabernacle (in Heaven), not made with hands, that is to say, not of this creation; [12] and not through the blood of goats and calves, but through His own blood, He entered the holy place (in Heaven) once for all, having obtained eternal redemption. [13] For if the blood of goats and bulls and the ashes of a heifer sprinkling those who have been defiled sanctify for the cleansing of the flesh, [14] how much more will the blood of Christ, who through the eternal Spirit offered Himself without blemish to God, cleanse your conscience from dead works to serve the living God?"

The word "verifies" at 1 John 5:6 and "verify" at verse 5:7 are both the word "Martureo" in the original Greek, which word means 'to bear witness.' And so again, what The Holy Spirit, the water, and the blood are in agreement as to the truth that Jesus Christ is indeed God's Son in human flesh. God adds at 1 John 5:6 that "it is the Spirit who testifies, because the Spirit is the truth." The water of baptism and the blood of the cross are both symbolic of unique events in time. However, The Holy Spirit is The third Person of The Godhead, that is, making up our One God, Who is on earth now to make real to believers the truth that God gave regarding His Son, Jesus Christ. Whereas The Son came to earth to make The Father known, The Holy Spirit is on earth now to make The Son known to believers! So there would be no value to the water baptism or the death on the cross of Jesus Christ unless He was indeed God's Son in human flesh, a truth that only The Holy Spirit can make known to believers in one's heart and mind as one reads this in God's word, thereby testifying to the truth of it.

The testimony of God The Father

In God having given us the testimony of The Spirit regarding His Son, God now turns to give believers His own testimony regarding His own Son at 1 John 5:9-13, "[9] **If we receive the testimony of men, the testimony of God is greater; for the testimony of God is this, that He has testified concerning His Son. [10] The one who believes in the Son of God has the testimony in himself; the one who does not believe God has made Him a liar, because he has not believed in the testimony that God has given concerning His Son. [11] And the testimony is this, that God has given us eternal life, and this life is in His Son. [12] He who has the Son has the life; he who does not have the Son of God does not have the life. [13] These things I have written to you who believe in the name of the Son of God, so that you may know that you have eternal life.**"

God's is pointing out here at verse 5:9 that human beings on earth are used to hearing the testimony that human beings might give, even about His own Son. However, we need to realize that God The Father also has given testimony regarding His Son, which, as can be expected, is far greater than human testimony, since Jesus Christ is His Son, Who has eternally dwelt with Him in His Presence in Heaven until such time as God The Father sent Him to earth to take on the body He had prepared for Him in the womb of the virgin (Hebrews 10:5). And so at 1 John 5:10, God says that the testimony that He gives regarding His Son is testimony that believers can testify to from the moment of their salvation onward, that is, from the moment of personally believing in God's Son, Jesus Christ, since each now has The Holy Spirit within to make that testimony a reality. On the other hand, unbelievers are liars, since they have denied the testimony that God has given of His Son in His word since the time of Adam and Eve, by not having believed the testimony that God The Father gave regarding His Son, Jesus Christ, in those Scriptures.

At 1 John 5:11 and the first part of verse 12, we have here the specific testimony that God The Father wants believers to know regarding His Son, Jesus Christ, which is that "...God has given us eternal life, and this life is in His Son. He who has the Son has the life..." And so that is why God adds at verse 5:13, "These things I have written to you who believe in the name of the Son of God, so that you may know that you have eternal life." What God is doing here is giving believers the assurance that they have eternal life with Him, which is forever, for having believed "in the name of the Son of God," which is Jesus Christ. To believe this is to have placed one's faith in God that all He said in His word regarding His Son is true, specifically the truth relating to His death for our sins, His burial, and His resurrection from the dead the third day, as we have already noted from 1 Corinthians 15:1-4, which is the basis for our having received the forgiveness of sins and eternal life with God. However, as God makes clear in the last part of 1 John 5:12, unbelievers on the other hand do not have eternal life with God, since they are those who do "not have The Son of God," and so do "not have the life," that is, eternal life with God, which is impossible to have apart from believing in the name of God's Son, Jesus Christ!

What God is sharing here is a truth that He has already shared, although in different words, in the first two verses of this first letter to believers through John, namely at 1 John 1:1,2, "[1] What was from the beginning, what we have heard, what we have seen with our eyes, what we have looked at and touched with our hands, concerning the Word of Life – [2] and the life was manifested, and we have seen and testify and proclaim to you the eternal life, which was with the Father and was manifested to us," when we believed in God's Son, Jesus Christ, for salvation. As already stated a number of times in the book so far, at the moment of our salvation, we received The Holy Spirit in our spirit, Who imparted to us God's own life, which is His righteous life, or righteousness, which is eternal life, this is true. However, what is also true is that God cannot be separated or divided.

What that means is that when we receive The Holy Spirit at salvation, we in fact receive The Son and The Father, Who also indwells us, since God is One (1 Timothy 2:5), noting here what God's Son told His followers at John 14:23, as those who believed in Him, "Jesus answered and said to him, "If anyone loves Me, he will keep My word; and My Father will love him, and We will come to him and make Our abode with him." " So that is why God The Father can say that he who has The Son has the life, since the life is in His Son, which one also receives when one receives The Holy Spirit at salvation. And that is why the apostle Paul could say at Galatians 2:20, "I have been crucified with Christ; and it is no longer I who live, but Christ lives in me; and the life which I now live in the flesh I live by faith in the Son of God, who loved me and gave Himself up for me."

The confidence that God wants believers to have in prayer

Then at 1 John 5:14,15, God again brings up a truth which He has already touched upon at 1 John 3:19-22, again using different words to express that truth, as we now see, "[14] **This is the confidence which we have before Him, that, if we ask anything according to His will, He hears us. [15] And if we know that He hears us in whatever we ask, we know that we have the requests which we have asked from Him.**" Since God is our Father and we are His children, then it only stands to reason that He would delight to hear us talk to Him about our needs on earth, or whatever concerns us; and that He would delight to answer our prayers, since He has all power at His disposal, which why He discloses of Himself at Matthew 19:26, "…with God all things are possible." The only thing that God cannot do is sin!

And so, at verse 5:14 here, God wants believers yet on earth to have confidence to approach Him with our requests, but making the stipulation that "if we ask anything according to His will, He hears us." Since God makes His will known to believers in His word, He is therefore saying here that our requests to Him need to be in line with His word, which is the expression of His will for His own yet on earth. What this means then is that before we ask God something, we need to ask ourselves if what we are asking is in line with God's word, to ensure that that what we are asking does not contravene His word.

Let us look at an example here that will make this truth clear to us. Let us say that we are married, and we ask God for a second spouse, where God calls for one woman for one man in marriage and vice-versa. Since this request is contrary to God's word, and therefore His will, then we can be sure that it is not one which He will answer. On the other hand, if what we want to ask God in prayer is in line with His will, since it is contained in His word, then we can have the confidence within ourselves in coming to God with that request, not only that He hears us, but also, as He goes on to add at verse 5:15, namely that, "if we know that He hears us in whatever we ask, we know that we have the requests which we have asked from Him."

Let us note some specific examples to help us here, noting what God tells believers at Philippians 4:6, "Be anxious for nothing, but in everything by prayer and supplication with thanksgiving let your requests be made known to God," and also at 1 Peter 5:7, "casting all your anxiety on Him, because He cares for you." Since God Himself calls believers to not be anxious about anything, but instead to give to Him in prayer the things that would tend to make us anxious in our moment by moment walk with Him, therefore, those are things that are part of His will and which we can ask for in confidence. And there are many other examples where God makes His will known in His word, which are legitimate things to pray about. If any reader would like to read more about prayer, the author has a book specifically on that subject, which is titled, "God Never Meant Prayer To Be A Mystery!"

Interceding with God on behalf of believers who sin

At 1 John 5:16,17, God calls believers to intercede with Him on behalf of other believers who we see commit a sin, noting what He there says, "[16} **If anyone sees his brother committing a sin not**

leading to death, he shall ask and God will for him give life to those who commit sin not leading to death. There is a sin leading to death; I do not say that he should make request for this. [17] **All unrighteousness is sin, and there is a sin not leading to death.**" The obvious two questions which present themselves here as one reads these words from God are: 1) Who is the "brother" in view here; a believer or anyone we encounter, including unbelievers? And 2) What is the "sin leading to death" that God has in view here?

To begin with the second question first, we are to see that the word "sin' is singular here, which means that there is only one such instance of sin leading to death, which God has in view here. And that sin is one that God warns believers about at 1 Corinthians 11:27-30, where we read, "[27] Therefore whoever eats the bread or drinks the cup of the Lord in an unworthy manner, shall be guilty of the body and the blood of the Lord. [28] But a man must examine himself, and in so doing he is to eat of the bread and drink of the cup. [29] For he who eats and drinks, eats and drinks judgment to himself if he does not judge the body rightly. [30] For this reason many among you are weak and sick, and a number sleep" (that is, have died physically).

So, what God is saying here is that any believer who partakes of The Lord's Supper, that is, communion, in an unworthy manner, which would refer to partaking of the elements of the bread and the cup while one has known unconfessed sins in one's life, then such a person is making a mockery of the sacrifice that God's Son, The Lord Jesus Christ, made on behalf of sinners, including that person. And so God says that person immediately comes under God's judgment, with God meting out His judgment as He sees fit, that being to allow some bodily condition to affect the believer who has sinned this way, or some illness, or even death as allowed by God.

What is likely here, as to what God allows to happen, is based on whether the believer is a new believer with not much knowledge, both in regards to how to take communion properly, that is, with no known unconfessed sins in one's life, or else in not knowing about the need of confessing one's sins to God directly, as we have seen at 1 John 1:9. In the case of a believer having the knowledge of both and yet sins in this way, the likely outcome is death at God's Hand, which is not necessarily a bolt of lightning from Heaven, but it could be any way that death may come, such as a stroke, cancer, an accident, etc. The only distinction here is that it part of God's judgment for sin.

So God says that if we see a believer sin such a sin on a Sunday, we are not to pray to Him on behalf of that believer. And of course, this presumes that we know for sure that this believer has sinned and has not confessed to God, which is almost impossible to know for sure. However, if one suspects that this is the case and one knows the person really well, one can go and speak with the "brother" afterwards regarding the need to come to the communion table with no known unconfessed sins in one's life, or one can go to one of the minister's of the local church and mention it to him. Any minister raised of God to be a minister would be aware of this sin and would be careful to advise beforehand those partaking of the elements that they need to partake with no known unconfessed sins in one's life, and then allow a few minutes for people to examine themselves, as God says at 1 Corinthians 11:28 that any believer planning to partake is supposed to do, simply because it can be a sin that leads to death!

Then as to the first question, we are to see that the word "brother" here refers to another believer, which of course means male or female. There is a very good reason for saying that here, which is based on what God says at verse 5:16 regarding such a "brother," who we see committing a sin not leading to death, in that believers are to pray to God on behalf of that person and "God will for him give life to those who commit a sin not leading to death." When God speaks of "life" here, He is not speaking of salvation, but rather He is speaking of continuing to have The Holy Spirit in that person's spirit continue to have His life imparted for that person to live by, which sin would normally interrupt. What this means then is that since only believers have The Holy Spirit indwelling within for that to happen, then this further means that the "brother" in view here is a believer!

And here God has in view any sin that is a sin, which is not the sin that leads to death. Again, what is most likely here is that the believer is a fairly new believer and may not know that certain words or practices are sin, so that one older in the faith who observes this might pray on one's behalf and God will forgive the sin and allow that person to continue with Him, since the person is yet a babe in Christ (noting 1 Corinthians 3:1-3) and has not yet been instructed regarded what is sin or not sin. Let us give some examples here to make this clearer. It is a fact that new believers are still very much caught up in living by one's sinful nature, so that there might at times be profanities still heard from them, or slander, and so forth, not knowing that these things are sin, until one has been instructed in the local church or until one has read in God's word that this is sin, with The Holy Spirit then convicting the person of sin once one knows the truth. But until then, believers who are more mature in the faith can pray to God for such believers when they hear them talk or see them act in ways that one knows is a sin.

When God says at 1 John 5:17 here, "all unrighteousness is sin," He is referring to the fact that all that comes from our sinful nature is sin. In other words, a believer is either living by God's own imparted life or righteousness moment by moment, or else a believer is living out of one's sinful nature, which is unrighteousness, since not coming from God as righteousness! And this includes all that one thinks, says, or does, while under the control of the sinful nature, since it is all sin or unrighteousness in God's sight.

No true believer practices sin, since God keeps His own from doing so!

Then God goes on at 1 John 5:18,19 to remind believers of another truth that He has already mentioned, but again using different words to do so, as we now see, "[18] **We know that no one who is born of God sins; but He who was born of God keeps him, and the evil one does not touch him. [19] We know that we are of God, and that the whole world lies in the power of the evil one.**" What should be clear to anyone reading what God says at verse 5:18 here, "We know that no one who is born of God sins," is that God is speaking of the practice of sin, as we have seen dealt with at 1 John 3:4-10. That this is the case here is due to the fact that all believers sin after salvation due to still having a sinful nature until the time of glorification, that is, until such time as one has that sinful nature removed when one experiences one's part in the first resurrection, when one enters God's Presence in Heaven to be with Him forever, where nothing sinful can ever enter. Besides, we should remember how God started 1 John 2, by saying to believers, "My little children, I am writing these things to you so that you may not sin. And if anyone sins, we have an Advocate with the Father, Jesus Christ the righteous…" So since believers can and do sin after salvation, then it should be clear to everyone that God has the 'practice' of sin in view here!

And so God continues and says at verse 5:18, "We know that no one who is born of God (that is, born into His family spiritually by The Holy Spirit at the moment of one's salvation, practices) sins; but He who was born of God (in the same way, that is, God's Son, Who although never needed to be saved, nevertheless did receive The Holy Spirit in taking on a human body and did live only by God's imparted life by The Holy Spirit while on earth) keeps him, and the evil one (that being the devil) does not touch him." In other words, God's Son keeps believers from practicing sin, because He knows that they are now God's children and therefore belong to His Father as part of the same family as He is Head over.

Let us note what God's Son prayed to His Father at John 17:1,2,6,12, which will give us an idea of what is involved here in the keeping power of God, [1] Jesus spoke these things; and lifting up His eyes to heaven, He said, "Father, the hour has come; glorify Your Son, that the Son may glorify You, [2] even as You gave Him authority over all flesh, that to all whom You have given Him, He may give eternal life… [6] I have manifested Your name to the men whom You gave Me out of the world; they were Yours and You gave them to Me, and they have kept Your word… [12] While I was with them, I was keeping them in Your name which You have given Me; and I guarded them and not one of them perished but the son of perdition, so that the Scripture would be fulfilled." In a similar way now, God's Son is keeping all believers from the practice of sin, since they all belong to God and He is guarding them from Heaven, so that the devil can no longer lead them to practice sin, as what they did when they were unbelievers. Believers can still sin, but not continue in sin without conviction of The Holy Spirit leading to confession.

As God goes on to say at 1 John 5:19, all believers are of God, in terms of having become so by God's grace and power in salvation, while "the whole world," meaning all the unbelievers of this present world, are "in the power of the evil one," that is, all yet belong to the devil, as we have seen at 1 John 3:9,10 already. Only God can free us from the power of the evil one, which He does at the moment of our salvation (of our believing in His Son), noting here what God says at Colossians 1:12,13, "[12] giving thanks to the Father, who has qualified us to share in the inheritance of the saints in Light. [13] For He rescued us from the domain of darkness, and transferred us to the kingdom of His beloved Son..." The children of God are those who cannot practice sin, although still able to sin due to still having a sinful nature, which the devil likes to tempt believers to act out of. The children of the devil are all unbelievers of the world who can only act out of one's sinful nature, since they do not know God, which means that all they practice at all times is sin, not being under the protective shield of God's Son, Jesus Christ, like believers are!

Believers are to guard themselves from the idols of this world, now that one personally knows God through His Son, Jesus Christ

Then we note that God closes this letter and His consolidation of truth in this chapter, by now saying to believers yet on earth at 1 John 5:20,21, "[20] **And we know that the Son of God has come, and has given us understanding so that we may know Him who is true; and we are in Him who is true, in His Son Jesus Christ. This is the true God and eternal life.** [21] **Little children, guard yourselves from idols.**" Believers are those yet on earth who know experientially within themselves from the moment of salvation onwards that one personally knows God, and that God's Son has indeed come from Heaven to earth in human flesh as Jesus Christ, and now also have the knowledge of Him as made known by The Holy Spirit in one's spirit, Who takes God's word, which testifies to God's Son, and makes that real to our hearts and minds. This therefore means that believers now personally know The true God, which assures one of indeed having eternal life with God (noting John 17:3).

And since believers now have eternal life with God due to being part of His eternal family as His children, then believers are to guard themselves from idols. The word "idols" here is "Eidolon" in the original and refers to the worship of any false gods apart from God. The reason that God mentions this to believers here is because He wants to remain not only at the center of our worship, but also at the center of our affections, and so not allow anything in this world to become more important to us than God! Let us note what God's Son said at Luke 14:26, "If anyone comes to Me, and does not hate his own father and mother and wife and children and brothers and sisters, yes, and even his own life, he cannot be My disciple." The word "hate" here means loving these more than God. So believers are to love and serve God above anyone or anything in this world. Turning from idols is again one thing that distinguishes believers from unbelievers, noting what God says to believers at 1 Thessalonians 1:9, "For they themselves report about us what kind of a reception we had with you, and how you turned to God from idols to serve a living and true God…"

As we close this first short letter from God to believers through John, we should briefly look at a comment made in the introduction to this letter in the first chapter, which is as follows: "However, we do know that it was the apostle John whom God chose to write down His word for us as believers in these three short letters simply from the internal evidence in the letters themselves, as we will see." And so, the 'internal evidence' here is simply the fact that over and over again in this letter we have made reference to the gospel account that God had John write down, so that John's gospel account was John being used of God to record the words and works of His Son while He was on earth, with First John being then, as is also true of all the other letters of the New Testament, God simply expanding in greater detail on what He said through His Son by The Holy Spirit while His Son was on earth.

SECTION 2
Second John

CHAPTER ONE

Second John 1:1-13

Introductory greeting and remarks from God through John

As we begin God's second short letter to believers through John, known as "Second John," we note that God gives an introductory greeting and some remarks at 2 John 1:1-4, "[1] **The elder to the chosen lady and her children, whom I love in truth; and not only I, but also all who know the truth, [2] for the sake of the truth which abides in us and will be with us forever: [3] Grace, mercy and peace will be with us, from God the Father and from Jesus Christ, the Son of the Father, in truth and love. "[4] I was very glad to find *some* of your children walking in truth, just as we have received commandment *to do* from the Father."** The word "elder" here is "Presbuteros" in the original, which can refer to both one who is advanced in years, or to one who is raised of God as part of the leadership of a local church.

Here the apostle John, who again has been chosen by God to write down this letter, uses the word "elder" to refer to himself as one who is aged. We know this from the use of the definite article "the" here. If God wanted to refer to John as an elder in a local church, He would have led John to write as when Peter referred to himself as a church elder at 1 Peter 5:1, "Therefore, I exhort the elders among you, as your fellow elder and witness of the sufferings of Christ, and a partaker also of the glory that is to be revealed..." We are to remember that a local church elder is never singular, but is always of a plurality of men raised of God, for God to minister through them to the gathered believers, noting Acts 14:23 and Titus 1:5. Nevertheless, John was still one who had high authority in the church of God (noting Galatians 2:9) and who had been chosen of Him to write down five New Testament letters, as we have noted.

We further note that God is here leading John to write "to the chosen lady and her children," which needs to be seen as not being a believing woman and her personal offspring here; but rather a local church and the believers who are a part of it, whom the apostle John was personally familiar with. The word "chosen" is "Eklektos" in the original Greek the New Testament was given in to mankind by God, and here refers to those elect of God unto salvation, as those God has personally chosen and then saved for Himself out of all who were going to a lost eternity. Let us note two passages where the same word is used to further help us grasp the meaning, the first being at Colossians 3:12, "So, as those who have been chosen (Eklektos) of God, holy and beloved, put on a heart of compassion, kindness, humility, gentleness and patience...," and the second being at 2 Timothy 2:10, "For this reason I endure all things for the sake of those who are chosen (Eklektos), so that they also may obtain the salvation which is in Christ Jesus and with it eternal glory."

The word "lady" is "Kuria" in the original, and here, and as already mentioned above, is a metaphorical reference to a local church then in existence. Similarly with the word "children", which is "Teknon," and here also applied metaphorically to the believers making up the local church that God is addressing this letter to. This is a local church which the apostle John was personally familiar with as he says, "whom I love in truth;" then adding, "and not only I, but also all who know the truth." All those who are saved, that is, who personally know God in salvation, are those who "know the truth."

And so, as we have seen mentioned a number of times by God in His First short letter through John, all those who are part of the family of God will love all the other members of the family of God, which here means that the believers of each local church will love all the other believers in each of the other local churches on earth. God then adds at 2 John 1:2 that this is so "for the sake of the truth which abides in us and will be in us forever." That word "truth," used by God four times in these first four verses, is "Atheleia" in the original and here speaks of the truth of God which has always existed with God and which came to mankind through God's Son, when He came to earth in human flesh.

In other words, God's Son, Jesus Christ, is the embodiment of the truth of God. Let us note what God says regarding that truth at John 1:14, "And the Word became flesh, and dwelt among us, and we saw His glory, glory as of the only begotten from the Father, full of grace and truth (Atheleia)," and also at Ephesians 4:21, "if indeed you have heard Him and have been taught in Him, just as truth (Atheleia) is in Jesus." Because God's Son continues with believers from the moment of salvation onward and forever by The Holy spirit in our spirit, then so will this be true in regards to the truth of God in us. Nobody can ever rob us of that truth, nor can we ever forget it, since it is God Who keeps believers in the that truth!

It is also to all believers that God adds at 2 John 1:3, "Grace, mercy, and peace will be with us, from God the Father and from Jesus Christ, the Son of the Father, in truth and love." As we see here, all the blessings that believers can ever receive in this life, in the next age, and for all eternity to come, comes to us from God The Father through His Son by The Holy Spirit in us, mentioning here "grace, mercy and peace" in particular, as what believers will have from God "in truth and love" from salvation onwards, forever and ever. God's grace is His unmerited favor upon believers; while His mercy is God forever withholding from believers what is due them due to one's sins; and peace, as the peace of God and with God, being the experience of believers forever. It is sure and it is undeserved by believers, simply coming to us because God is true to Himself, expressing His essential character to His own forever, which as we have seen is love (noting again 1 John 4:8,16, "God is love"). The love that comes to believers from God at salvation "always rejoices with the truth" (1 Corinthians 13:6).

What is interesting to note here is that God refers to His Son, not with the words 'God's Son,' as He has done a number of times in His first short letter through John, but rather here as "the Son of the Father." Here we have the family relationship being particularly emphasized, in that our One God consists of The Father and His Son, with The Holy Spirit not here being mentioned, but nevertheless understood, since, as just mentioned, the family relationship within the Godhead is here being emphasized by God. In this instance, God is not saying this as a test of whether one is a believer or not, based on whether one believes this or not; but rather is just stating a fact of what is, whether it is believed or not!

We also note that God says at 2 John 1:3, "and from Jesus Christ." However, we are to be aware that although God does not say here, 'through' Jesus Christ, nevertheless, we need to note what God says at John 1:3 in part, relating to His Son, The Lord Jesus Christ, "All things came into being through Him," then again at John 1:10 in part, "the world was made through Him,' and then again at 1 Corinthians 8:6, "yet for us there is but one God, the Father, from whom are all things and we exist for Him; and one Lord, Jesus Christ, by whom are all things, and we exist through Him" (see also Colossians 1:16 and Hebrews 1:2).

What we are to see here is that when God The Father acts or speaks, it is always through His Son by The Holy Spirit, whether that is specifically mentioned or not, noting what God's Son said while on earth at John 14:10,24 in parts, "[10] …the Father abiding in Me does His works… [24]…the word which you hear is not Mine, but the Father's who sent Me." So why does God say, "and from Jesus Christ," here then? Simply to emphasize the unity of God, in that even though there are three indivisible Persons in our One God, He does not act, or speak, as three separate Persons, but rather always as One God, which is always from God The Father through His Son by The Holy Spirit!

We further note God leads John to write down this letter, which must have been shortly after he had visited with this particular local church of believers, for he gives a personal eyewitness account at verse 1:4, "I was very glad to find…" And what the apostle John observed while there was that some of the believers were "walking in truth," but not all, and this must have affected him, which God knew, and the result was this letter; which like the rest of the New Testament and Old Testament, is the word of God (2 Timothy 3:16).

We need to notice that God then says here at 2 John 1:4, "walking in truth," and then recall that at Ephesians 4:21 we have seen that "just as truth is in Jesus," which means that believers need to walk as God's Son Himself walked while on earth, noting again 1 John 2:6, "the one who says he abides in Him (God's Son) ought himself to walk in the same manner as He walked." As John is led of God to write here, regarding "walking in truth," this is "just as we have received a commandment to do from the Father," noting what God tells us at Ephesians 5:1,2, "[1] Therefore be imitators of God, as beloved children; [2] and walk in love, just as Christ also loved you and gave Himself up for us, an offering and a sacrifice to God as a fragrant aroma." And if we walk with God as His Son, Jesus Christ, did while on earth, in love and in truth, then we will indeed be "walking in truth," since the love of God cannot exist or be manifested apart from the truth of God.

God now states two very important reasons why this second short letter was given

We now come to the two very important reasons for why God gave this second short letter to believers on earth through John, with the first reason being at 2 John 1:5,6, while the second reason is at 2 John 1:7-11. And so, let us note the first reason at verses 1:5,6, **[5] Now I ask you, lady, not as though *I were* writing to you a new commandment, but the one which we have had from the beginning, that we love one another. [6] And this is love, that we walk according to His commandments. This is the commandment, just as you have heard from the beginning, that you should walk in it.** Let us recall that we have noted already that "lady" here is the local church that the apostle John personally knows and has visited, and to which God is now writing to through him.

And what God wants to remind this local church is that "we love one another," something that was obviously missing in this local church and is really something that will not happen as long as believers are focusing on themselves and forget that each one was saved in order to serve God, which means putting His will first, before our own, which further means looking after God's interests while on earth! Let us note what God says at Philippians 2:2-4, of what will be seen among believers as we love one another, "[2] make my joy complete by being of the same mind, maintaining the same love, united in spirit, intent on one purpose. [3] Do nothing from selfishness or empty conceit, but with humility of mind regard one another as more important than yourselves; [4] do not merely look out for your own personal interests, but also for the interests of others."

As we also see here, John is led to say at verse 1:5 that this is "not a new commandment, but one which we have had from the beginning," that is, since the moment of one's salvation, God has been teaching that truth through His Holy Spirit as He came to indwell each believer. In other words, not only is loving one another as believers a sign that we are truly children of God, as we have seen, but it is also an indication of a believer walking with God. For as long as we are indeed walking by God's life imparted by The Holy Spirit when we have no known unconfessed sins in our lives, then the love of God is continuously flowing from us as believers to those around us! This is what God wants to see happen among the believers in each local church on earth.

Then God continues on a familiar theme at 2 John 1:6, when He says, "And this is love, that we walk according to His commandments..." We have already touched on this truth at 1 John 2:5 and also at 1 John 5:3, and again here point out that to "walk according to His commandments" identifies one as a child of God, since this means that one is obeying God, that is, is doing His will, which is expressed in His word. Only those who personally know God in salvation will ever do this. And when God says, "this is love," He is indicating that in order for this to be true in us, then we need to deny self so as to live for Him, which means loving God more than ourselves, since we are putting His will before ours. And what is very important for us to see here is that believers automatically do love God and are walking in obedience to His word when one walks with Him moment by moment with no known unconfessed sins in one's life!

When God goes on to say in the last part of verse 1:6, "This is the commandment, just as you have heard from the beginning (that is, from the moment of one's salvation), that you should walk in it," He is indicating that believers need to walk in accordance with God's word. In other words, His word is to guide our lives daily and is to be the basis for the practice of our life with God. Let us note what God says at Psalm 119:105, which is to be true of all believers, "Your word is a lamp to my feet and a light to my path." And so at 2 John 1:5,6 here, God is pointing out that some, in this local church here in view, were not walking in truth, in that they were not walking in love nor in truth because simply not walking in accordance to God's word. Let us note what God calls this at Revelation 2:4, "But I have this against you, that you have left your first love." In other words, 'you have stopped living in obedience to God's word, which means you have stopped loving God more than self, since you must love self more than God in now doing your own will instead of God's will, which you would be doing if you obeyed His word.'

118

And then, as mentioned above, the second reason that God states for giving believers this second short letter through John is found at verses 1:7-11, where we read, "[7] **For many deceivers have gone out into the world, those who do not acknowledge Jesus Christ as coming in the flesh. This is the deceiver and the antichrist.** [8] **Watch yourselves, that you do not lose what we have accomplished, but that you may receive a full reward.** [9] **Anyone who goes too far and does not abide in the teaching of Christ, does not have God; the one who abides in the teaching, he has both the Father and the Son.** [10] **If anyone comes to you and does not bring this teaching, do not receive him into your house, and do not give him a greeting;** [11] **for the one who gives him a greeting participates in his evil deeds.**"

We see here that God was concerned for the believers of this local church, both those who were walking with Him by walking by the truth of His word, and even those who were not due to having gone astray in some way, as He says here to these believers at verse 1:8, "Watch yourselves..." What God does not want to see happen to these believers, nor any believers anywhere, is to "lose what you have accomplished (since the moment of your salvation)," so that when your life here on earth is ended "you may receive a full reward" from God. God then goes on at 2 John 1:9 to pinpoint what will lead one to lose what one has accomplished by God's grace since salvation, and so cause one to lose one's reward with God, which is "anyone who goes too far and does not abide (that is, continue) in the teaching of Christ," referring here to not living in accordance with God's word. At 1 Corinthians 4:6 God expresses this as "learn not to exceed what is written" in God's word!

What we are also to observe from what God further says at verse 1:9 here is that to "abide in the teaching" of God's word is really another test of whether one is a believer or not, for "the one who abides in the teaching... has both the Father and the Son," and so is a believer; while the one "who does not abide in the teaching of Christ, does not have God," and so, is an unbeliever. What this means then is that believers will continue in the teaching of God's word. Why? Simply because one has been born into the family of God spiritually, and it is God by His Holy Spirit in the believer that causes one to live in accordance with His word, that is, to continue in the teaching!

We need to ever remember that salvation, and all our life afterwards as believers, is wholly a work of God's grace and power right up to the end of our lives on earth. And God cannot fail in this work. Let us note again what God says to believers at Philippians 1:6, "For I am confident of this very thing, that He (God) who began a good work in you (at salvation) will perfect it until the day of Christ Jesus," which is when we are finally with God in spirit, soul, and body, at the time of glorification. Another important verse in this regard is what God says at Ephesians 2:10, "For we are His workmanship, created in Christ Jesus (in reference to the moment of one's salvation) for good works, which God prepared beforehand so that we would walk in them." And let us also take to heart what God says relating to believers at Hebrews 13:21 in part, "(May God) ...equip you in every good thing to do His will, working in us that which is pleasing in His sight, through Jesus Christ..." Amen to that!

God continues His warning to believers at 2 John 1:10,11, by saying that "if anyone comes to you and does not bring this teaching," which would be the case if someone was teaching what was not in accordance with God's word; then believers are "not to receive him into your house, and do not give him a greeting" even, "for the one who gives him a greeting participates in his evil deeds." Let us remember what God said back at 1 John 2:15,17 in part, "[15] Do not love the world nor the things in the world. If anyone loves the world, the love of the Father is not in him... [17] the one who does the will of God (which is made known in His word) lives forever." There is no doubt that every person reading this has had to answer the door at one time or other and be faced with a person or persons trying to lead one to listen to a message or take some literature from them, which if examined carefully would not be in accordance with God's word, but would be from some cult that the devil has raised on earth to try to lead believers astray from God's word.

That is why God began this section by saying at 2 John 1:7, "For many deceivers have gone out into the world, those who do not acknowledge Jesus Christ as coming in the flesh. This is the deceiver and the antichrist." And that is also why God further warns believers at 2 Corinthians 11:14,15, "[14] No wonder, for even Satan disguises himself as an angel of light. [15] Therefore it is not surprising if his servants also disguise themselves as servants of righteousness, whose end will be according to their deeds." The devil and his human workers on earth do not come to us in wolf's clothing, but rather innocently in sheep's clothing, so as to try to deceive the unsuspecting. And so that is why God tells believers, "watch yourselves…"

We note that God again refers to unbelievers who oppose God, His word, and believers as "deceivers who have gone out into the world," simply because they are, knowingly or unknowingly, tools of the devil, with God concluding that thought by saying, "This is the deceiver and the antichrist." As we have seen at First John already, the devil is indeed the deceiver, as God says of him at Revelation 12:9 in part, "…the serpent of old who is called the devil and Satan, who deceives the whole world…" And coming on the world scene as ruler over the nations of the earth as soon as the present third age of time ends is the antichrist, who will be under the devil to oppose all that is of God on the earth, including believers. The devil and the antichrist "do not acknowledge Jesus Christ as coming in the flesh" due to being fallen angels, who have been left in their sins by God, which means that those who are unbelievers on earth, who are also all under the devil's control, will do the same.

So believers really do need to watch themselves, having their eyes fully open to what is going on in the world around them. We are not to worry, only to be aware. And we surely need to remember what God says at Romans 14:17,18, "[17] for the kingdom of God is not eating and drinking, but righteousness and peace and joy in the Holy Spirit. [18] For he who in this way serves Christ is acceptable to God and approved by men." It is good to remember once again that the "righteousness" that God has in view here is His life, which is imparted to us in the peace and joy of The Holy Spirit as we walk with God with no known unconfessed sins in our lives!

God's concluding remarks through John

God now concludes this second short letter through John by saying at 2 John 1:12,13, "[12] **Though I have many things to write to you, I do not want to do so with paper and ink; but I hope to come to you and speak face to face, so that your joy may be made full. [13] The children of your chosen sister greet you.**" We see here that the apostle John was limited in what to include in this short letter to only what God wanted to communicate to these believers at this time. The fact that God wanted this to be "with paper and ink" means that its message, as is true of the rest of the word of God contained in both the Old and New Testament portions of the Bible, was meant for the church universal, that is, was meant for all the believers in all the local churches on earth.

And if God did allow John to revisit that particular local church again, then whatever John would have shared additionally with them would be specific to that local church. In other words, it would not be inspired, since it would not be the word of God, but simply the counsel or words of wisdom from a church authority, which the apostle John was, to a particular group of believers. The reference to the believers of this local church having their joy made full by John being physically present with them simply means that he would then have an opportunity to teach them the revealed word of God, so that what was yet lacking in their knowledge of the truth of the faith might be made known to them.

And when John says here "The children of your chosen sister greet you," he is in effect saying that the believers of the local church where he was at presently - at the time that God was using him as His instrument to write down this letter – are sending their greetings to you there, as the believers of the local church this letter was coming to, before it made its way to the other local churches in existence as part of the New Testament. And so, "chosen sister" simply means similarly chosen, that is, elect of God for salvation as now believers making up the local church referred to here in the word "sister."

SECTION 3
Third John

CHAPTER ONE

Third John 1:1-15

God writes to one believer, but the message, since it is the word of God, is intended for all believers on earth

As we begin God's third short letter written to believers through the apostle John, known as "Third John," we note that God now writes to just one believer, although the message contained herein is for all believers, since this is the word of God. And so, God now says at 3 John 1:1 through John, "**The elder to the beloved Gaius, whom I love in truth.**" Again, we see John refer to himself as "the elder," which is again a reference to the fact that he is now an old man, as he is led of God to write this. It is possible that both Second and Third John were given by God at around the same time, and even while John was among the believers at the local church from which this was being written.

And here we note that this letter is "to the beloved Gaius," who was no doubt a believer, whom the apostle John personally knew from the past, since he adds here, "whom I love in truth." This man "Gaius" is mentioned four other times in God's word. From the first mention at Acts 19:29, we learn that Gaius was one of the apostle Paul's traveling companions, and that he was from Macedonia, which was a province of the Roman Empire encompassing most of northern Greece, "Gaius and Aristarchus, Paul's traveling companions from Macedonia." Then when we are given more information at Acts 20:4, we are there told that Gaius was actually from the city of Derbe in the Roman province of Galatia, and that it was only Aristarchus who was from Macedonia (Thessalonica being a city of Macedonia), as we there read, "And he (Paul) was accompanied by...Aristarchus and Secundus of the Thessalonians, and Gaius of Derbe..."

Then the third mention of "Gaius" in God's word, which are all references to the same believer, is at Romans 16:23, where God writes through the apostle Paul, "Gaius, host to me and to the whole church, greets you..." From this reference, it would appear that Gaius was a man of some financial means. The word "host" here is "Xenos" in the original and refers to one who receives and provides for other believers in a hospitable manner. This information will be very helpful as we proceed here in Third John. The fourth mention of "Gaius" is at 1 Corinthians 1:14, where the apostle Paul mentions that he was one of the few believers that he had baptized in water, most likely because he took him with him as a traveling companion and he had not yet been baptized as a believer; and not meaning here that Gaius had been one that he had led to faith in God. And then the final mention of "Gaius" is here at 3 John 1:1.

We learn that Gaius was a man that the apostle John had led to faith in God, and who was now still walking with God

We then learn from 3 John 1:2-4 that Gaius was a believer that the apostle John had personally led to faith in God, and that Gaius was still walking with God, even years later, "[2] **Beloved, I pray that in all respects you may prosper and be in good health, just as your soul prospers. [3] For I was very glad when brethren came and testified to your truth, that is, how you are walking in truth**. [4] **I have no greater joy than this, to hear of my children walking in the truth**." Here the apostle John is led of God to address Gaius as "Beloved," because as we have seen at verse 1:1 already, he was someone whom the apostle John loved in The Lord, that is, as a fellow believer of the same family of God that he was. And since this is God's word, we also see that it is God's will for believers to "be in good health," which is what the apostle John wished for Gaius here.

The word "prosper(s)" here is "Euodoo" in the original and in its first occurrence at 3 John 1:2 refers to one's external circumstances, such as in business; while in the second instance, where the word "prospers" is in reference to his "soul," which is his person, the reference is to his general wellbeing generally. John's love for his brother meant that he was concerned for his welfare in all areas of life! As we see at 3 John 1:3 here, that concern especially touched

126

the spiritual sphere of life, for if one does not know God, or if one is not "walking in truth," then all the money, power, health, and fame in the world will not avail much in the end. Life with God is what makes life worth living, which is why God's Son, The Lord Jesus Christ, declared at John 10:10, "The thief (that is, the devil) comes only to steal and kill and destroy; I came that they may have life, and have it abundantly."

We see from verse 1:3 here that in Gaius' case, he was indeed "walking in truth," as the apostle John has just had word from some believers that had recently been in contact with Gaius and they found it so. And it is at this point that we learn that it had been the apostle John who had actually been used of God to lead this man Gaius to faith in God through believing in His Son, The Lord Jesus Christ, when he says in a general way, "I have no greater joy than this, to hear of my children walking in the truth." The reference to "my children" here would be a reference to all those led to faith in God by John, which no doubt included Gaius.

Let us also note what God led the apostle Paul to write at 1 Corinthians 4:14,15 in this regard, "[14] I do not write these things to shame you, but to admonish you as my beloved children. [15] For if you were to have countless tutors in Christ, yet you would not have many fathers, for in Christ Jesus I became your father through the gospel." For John to be glad that Gaius was "walking in truth" here in the spiritual sphere would be equivalent to parents in the secular sphere being glad that their children were doing well and were successful in life after leaving home.

The reasons for why God gave this third short letter are now stated

As with every other letter from God in the New Testament, God has a reason for raising a servant of His to write down His thoughts so as to deal with whatever problem was occurring in His church on earth. Since human nature is the same, even from the time of Adam and Eve to the present, then whatever problems were encountered in the church among believers in the first century AD, when this letter was written, is still valid even today, in the twenty-first century AD! And so, we see from 3 John 1:5-12 here that John now brings up the matters that God is aware of, both good and evil, encouraging the good and denouncing the evil, as we now read, "[5] **Beloved, you** are acting faithfully in whatever you accomplish for the brethren, and especially when they are strangers; [6] and they have testified to your love before the church. You will do well to send them on their way in a manner worthy of God. [7] For they went out for the sake of the Name, accepting nothing from the Gentiles. [8] Therefore we ought to support such men, so that we may be fellow workers with the truth. [9] I wrote something to the church; but Diotrephes, who loves to be first among them, does not accept what we say. [10] For this reason, if I come, I will call attention to his deeds which he does, unjustly accusing us with wicked words; and not satisfied with this, he himself does not receive the brethren, either, and he forbids those who desire to do so and puts them out of the church. [11] Beloved, do not imitate what is evil, but what is good. The one who does good is of God; the one who does evil has not seen God. [12] Demetrius has received a good testimony from everyone, and from the truth itself; and we add our testimony, and you know that our testimony is true."

From 3 John 1:5-8, we see that God starts by commending Gaius by encouraging him to continue to do the good that he was doing as part of the local church he was there associated with. What we see occurring here is that some male believers (verse 8, "such men"), who were part of the local church that the apostle John was associated with, left there to go to the local church that Gaius was a part of. Now these men have returned to their own local church and have reported what has occurred on their journey, which included the good and the evil recorded here. The good was that Gaius had helped these men greatly, which means again that he appears to have been a believer of substantial financial means.

However, the evil that these men encountered was that there was another man in the local church there by the name of "Diotrephes," whom Gaius would no doubt have been aware of, who did "not receive the brethren" and even "forbids those who desire to do so and puts them out of the church" (verse 10). The apostle John had sent a letter (verse 9, "I wrote something to the church"), but this man Diotrephes, "does not accept what we say," with the "we" here being a reference to the fact that the apostle John had written that letter, but it had been on behalf of the local church he was a part of. And because of the adverse reaction that the men had encountered from

Diotrephes, including the ungodly dealings with the believers of the local church who did not agree with his actions and who themselves wanted to help the visiting brothers, this then necessitated this letter from John to Gaius, whom God knew could be relied upon as a faithful servant of His there.

The visiting brothers did also mention to their local church, which included John, that they had encountered a man there by the name of "Demetrius," whom John mentions at verse 12, who "received a good testimony from everyone," relating to those in the local church he was part of and also from the visiting brothers. And so, we are to see here that in God saying to Gaius through John at verse 11 here, "Beloved, do not imitate what is evil, but what is good. The one who does good is of God; the one who does evil has not seen God," He is letting Gaius know that Demetrius has God's approval as a believer, while Diotrephes did not, being seen as an unbeliever, judging by his words, "unjustly accusing us with wicked words," and by his actions, "not satisfied with this, he himself does not receive the brethren, either, and he forbids those who desire to do so and puts them out of the church" (verse 10).

What we are to see about this man "Diotrephes" then is that he appears to have been a self-appointed leader of the local church there, where Gaius was attending. As an unbeliever, he would have disregarded God's word regarding the appointment of elders for each local church, namely that it was to be a plurality of two or more men, including the qualifications that God says such men must have, noting 1 Timothy 3:1-7 here, "[1] It is a trustworthy statement: if any man aspires to the office of overseer, it is a fine work he desires to do. [2] An overseer, then, must be above reproach, the husband of one wife, temperate, prudent, respectable, hospitable, able to teach, [3] not addicted to wine or pugnacious, but gentle, peaceable, free from the love of money. [4] He must be one who manages his own household well, keeping his children under control with all dignity [5] (but if a man does not know how to manage his own household, how will he take care of the church of God?), [6] and not a new convert, so that he will not become conceited and fall into the condemnation incurred by the devil. [7] And he must have a good reputation with those outside the church, so that he will not fall into reproach and the snare of the devil."

If we compare this list with what we are told of Diotrephes at 3 John, we could say that he was not above reproach, was not respectable, was not hospitable, was not peaceable, and certainly did not have a good reputation with those outside the church. But what most disqualified him was the fact that he was not even a believer, so should not even have been part of the local church there, since a local church in God's sight is all the believers in a community. For instance, when God wrote to the local church at Philippi, another Roman colony of the first century AD, He said through the apostle Paul at verses 1:1 of that letter, "Paul and Timothy, bond-servants of Christ Jesus, to all the saints (that is, all those who are) in Christ Jesus (being therefore believers) who are in Philippi, including the overseers and deacons:"

What God appears to want to see happen here then is for Gaius to gather the believers there, once he has this letter from God through John known as "Third John," and together as a local church to expel Diotrephes from their midst and appoint Demetrius as part of the eldership in his place, thereby restoring order to that local church. This may well have been the reason why the visiting brothers had first been sent from the local church where John was to this local church experiencing these problems, to investigate and report back as to what the true conditions there were.

The fact that we are told at verse 7 regarding these visiting brothers, "For they went out for the sake of the Name, accepting nothing from the Gentiles," have led some to think, from just a superficial reading of this letter, that these were likely evangelists, who were going out from their local church, being supported only by the contributions of believers, and never accepting money from unbelievers (the "Gentiles" here). This is something that was examined and thoroughly discounted in my book, "Evangelism As God Intended." It is, however, true that God desires the work of the local churches on earth to be funded by God's people, and not by unbelievers.

Concluding remarks

God concludes His letter to these believers through John in a manner very similar to the way He ended Second John, as we now see from 3 John 1:13-15, "**[13] I had many things to write to you, but I am not willing to write them to you with pen and ink; [14] but I hope to see you shortly, and we will speak face to face. [15]**

Peace be to you. The friends greet you. Greet the friends by name." When the apostle John says at verse 13 that he had many things to write to Gaius, but does not want to do it as part of this letter, he is indicating that whatever else he has to say to his friend and brother in The Lord is of a human nature and therefore not the inspired word of God. In other words, just as we have noted at the end of Second John, the apostle John could only write what God in him was leading him to write while under the total control of The Holy Spirit to accurately and completely communicate the eternal world of God!

That is why John can say at verse 14 that he hopes to see Gaius shortly and then will be in a position to speak with him these other thoughts that he personally would like to speak to him about, doing so now face to face. Speaking face to face would not be a recorded conversation as it now is in writing, which has been preserved for almost 2000 years by God as His eternal word to mankind. And then verse 15 is again the believers of the local church where John is sending greetings to the believers of the local church where Gaius is. What is interesting here is that the closing now is simply, "Peace to you," which is not surprising since the events taking place at the local church where Gaius is would have indeed experienced anything but peace, due to the presence and actions of this unbeliever Diotrephes, who had been doing nothing but serving the devil's purposes while sowing chaos in God's body of believers there.

To God alone be all praise, honor, and glory, with thanksgiving, both now and forevermore! Amen, amen, and amen.

"Jesus said to him, "I am the way, and the truth, and the life; no one comes to the Father but through Me." "

John 14:6

ADDENDUM A

/ The four ages of time

What is important to know when reading God's word, the Bible, is that God has divided time into four ages. And since God's word covers all of time, then all of God's word, the Bible, can be subdivided along the lines of these four ages. But before noting what these four ages are, we need to also be aware that in each of the four ages of time, God uses the believers of that age as His vessels. In other words, God is accomplishing His work on earth through the believers of each age of time. And what is also important to keep in mind in regards to this is that although God starts each age with believers, before long the number of unbelievers in each age outnumbers the number of believers. In other words, one characteristic of each age of time is that there is a believing remnant among a mass of unbelievers, with these believers in each age being those whom God preserves for Himself and through whom God works to accomplish His purposes in each age through time.

And so in the first age of time, God worked through Adam and his believing descendants as His vessels to accomplish His will on earth, which age covers the first eleven chapters of Genesis. What this means is that they were the believers who willingly served Him out of love for Him. In other words, this was the believing line of descent, or the believing remnant, through which God worked out His will. Then when we begin Genesis 12, we see God take one believer, Abraham, and out of that one man's descendants through the line of Isaac, and then through the line of Jacob, God makes a nation, which is Israel. And again, we need to see that only the believing line of descent within the nation of Israel was the remnant through which God worked to accomplish His will. What this means is that not all those who were of the nation of Israel were believers. In fact, the majority were unbelievers. Therefore, in the second age of time, which goes from Genesis 12 to the end of Malachi in the Old Testament, and includes the gospel accounts of Matthew, Mark, Luke, and John, plus Acts 1 and Revelation 6 to 19 in the New Testament, God works out His will in time through the believers of the nation of Israel, which is again a small number compared to the total number.

And here we need to pause for a moment and mention something else before going on to consider the third age of time, and this is the fact of representation. What this means is that in the first age of time, we have Adam and Eve as our first parents, who were but representative of all people on earth. In other words, God knew that what this one couple did, any other couple would have done the same thing, since God knows that once sin entered His perfect and sinless creation, we all would have the same sinful nature as human beings. Then the same is true in regards to the nation of Israel in the second age of time, in that God knew that what this one nation did, any other nation on earth would likewise have done had it been chosen by God as a representative nation. So when God set out to make the one nation of Israel, He started out with just believers. But when the nation of Israel came into existence later, only a believing remnant within the nation were believers. Now since the nation of Israel was but representative of all the nations, then God knew that if He had chosen any other nation on earth, He would find that only a believing remnant would ever become believers to serve Him willingly out of love for Him out of a mass of unbelievers who would not in any of those nations also. In other words, no other human being would have acted any differently than our first parents, and likewise, no other nation would have acted any differently than the nation of Israel did. This means that all human beings and all nations are likewise guilty before God.

What also needs to be mentioned here as we now go on to look at the third age of time, is that the first two ages basically cover the time period covered by the Old Testament, which means that the remaining third and fourth ages of time must be covered by the New Testament portion of God's word, the Bible. And let us recall that in the first age, God worked through the believers of that age, beginning with Adam, while in the second age of time, God works through the believers of the nation of Israel, beginning with Abraham. So as we come to the third age of time, which goes from Acts 2 to the end of Revelation 5 in God's word, the Bible, we have God working through the believers of earth, whom God calls "the church." What this means then is that in this third age of time, which we are presently still in, God is accomplishing His will through all the believers of earth, with God now not looking at any specific nation in particular. In other words, during the present third age of time, also known as the church age, the nation of Israel, although being supernaturally preserved by God, is still just the same as any other nation on earth, having a believing remnant among a majority of unbelievers.

Then in the fourth age of time, which is basically covered by Revelation 20 to 22 in the New Testament, although mentioned often in prophecy in various portions of the Old Testament, we have God working through the believers of that age, but now with much greater variation. In other words, during the fourth age of time God works through the believers of every nation on earth still in their natural bodies and also through the believers of the first three ages of time, who would have experienced their part in the first resurrection relating to believers and who are now in their resurrected bodies. This is covered in much greater detail in my book, "An Introduction To The New World That Is Coming Upon The Earth," which focuses on this fourth age of time. If there are any readers who are not sure of what is meant by the first and second resurrection and the fact of people serving God in their new resurrected bodies in the future, please see my book, "Have You Ever Wondered What Happens After Death?"

Before leaving this Addendum, it is also important to be aware that the Old Testament portion of God's word, the Bible, contains 39 books, which deal with the beginning of all things in God's plan of the ages, while the New Testament portion of God's word, the Bible, contains 27 books, which deal with the consummation of all things in God's eternal plan, which God is outworking through the four ages of time. Also of great value is knowing that the second age of time is not completed until AFTER the completion of the present third age of time. In other words, there are seven years remaining in the second age of time dealing with the nation of Israel, which is why this nation is being supernaturally preserved by God during this present third age, simply because God is not yet finished outworking His plan of the ages through that nation. This seven years remaining is a time of

God's judgment against all unbelievers of earth and is approximately covered by Revelation 6:1 to Revelation 19:21 in God's word, although also mentioned often in prophecy in the Old Testament.

What also needs to be mentioned and is important to remember is that the reason God has a series of ages in time is in order to show us just how sinful the human race is and just how incapable it is of doing good, in terms of pleasing God on its own apart from God. What is meant here is that God's revelation of Himself increases as time progresses, so that those living in the fourth age of time as compared to the first age of time will have a far greater knowledge of God. In other words, as each age progresses, God makes it easier and easier for human beings on earth to come to know Him and to serve Him out of love for Him. For example, in the first two ages, God's precious Son had not yet come to earth, so that He was represented only through types, such as the animal sacrifices, and in prophecy. Human beings at that time also only had the Old Testament as light to guide them.

But by the time we reach the fourth age of time, God's precious Son will not only have come from Heaven to earth bodily, but will actually be on earth reigning over the nations as King. Please note what God says at Isaiah 11:9 in part, as just one example, "...For the earth will be full of the knowledge of the Lord as the waters cover the sea." What this means then is that when God's final judgment of time comes, relating to all the unbelievers of time (Revelations 20:11-15), then none of these unbelievers of time will be able to stand before God and give any excuse for their sin of unbelief, in having personally and freely rejected God's offer of salvation found in His own precious Son, Jesus Christ. And so each succeeding age adds to mankind's culpability before a Holy and altogether Righteous God so that in the end "every mouth may be closed and all the world may become accountable to God" (Romans 3:19 in part).

ADDENDUM B

/ The two comings from Heaven to earth of God's precious Son, our Lord Jesus Christ

Another very important truth to know here is that God's word, the Bible, mentions two comings of God's precious Son, Jesus Christ, from Heaven to earth. His first coming from Heaven to earth was for the purpose of taking on a body like ours, only in the innocence of Adam and as born of a virgin so as not to incur our sinful nature, and then after living thirty-three and half years on earth carrying out only the will of God His Father in absolute sinlessness out of love for Him, was given over into the hands of unbelievers to be put to death on a cross, before being buried, then resurrected from the dead the third day. And of course, His death was not due to anything God's precious Son, our Lord Jesus Christ, had ever done wrong, but rather was to pay the penalty due our sins, which was death, in order that God might have a basis by which to forgive the sins of those who believe in Him.

Then the second coming of God's precious Son is to be seen as being in two stages. The first stage of His second coming is at the end of this present third age of time, and is for the purpose of bringing to Heaven all believers of earth before God's judgment falls on the unbelievers of the earth, thereby bringing the present third age to a close. God has this first stage in view especially at 1 Thessalonians 4:14-17, although also mentioned in many portions of the New Testament. Then the second stage of the second coming of God's precious Son, Jesus Christ, occurs at the end of the seven years of God's judgment and will end the second age of time. God's precious Son would now be coming for one last battle against God's foes, as led by the devil, before establishing His reign on earth as King during the fourth age of time. This is again disclosed by God in many portions of God's word in the New Testament, but especially in passages such as Matthew 24:29,30 and Revelation 19:11-21.

Therefore, as we next turn to look at the subject matter of this book proper it is good to remember all that we have just looked at in Addendum A and B as background information and as a foundation for what we are now going to look at in the rest of the book. If there are any readers who would like more detailed information about the two comings of God's precious Son from Heaven to earth, or of the prophecies such as Daniel 9:24-27 relating to it, then one may want to consult the author's book, already mentioned, which is, "An Introduction To The New World That Is Coming Upon The Earth." All the author's books are available as a print copy and as an eBook for any type of eReaders.

ADDENDUM C

/ For those who may not as yet know God

Possibly you have been reading this book and have become aware of not knowing this God Who created us and gave us physical life into this world, and up to now has allowed you to live on earth. However, you do have the desire to know God in a personal way. If this is the case, then this chapter has been written specifically for you. And what God wants you to have in coming to know Him is the peace and joy which comes in knowing that all of your sins committed in your lifetime are forgiven and that you have eternal life with God. And so, your greatest need at the moment is to make peace with God so as to go to Heaven, which is God's eternal home. And so this chapter will help to bring that about by pointing you to God so as to come to faith in Him.

And as we begin, we need to note a most important promise which God makes at Romans 6:23 to all those who do not yet know Him, "For the wages of sin is death, but the free gift of God is eternal life in Christ Jesus our Lord." The good news here is that God offers you eternal life with Him as a free gift, which is to be obtained in His Son, Jesus Christ. What God does not do in this verse from the Bible is tell us how to obtain that eternal life with Him. Another verse which we can look at where God does let us know how one can obtain that eternal life with Him is noting what God tells us at John 3:16, "For God so loved the world, that He gave His only begotten Son, that whoever believes in Him shall not perish, but have eternal life." Now the added truth which God makes known here is that the eternal life, which He gives to a human being as a free gift, is for those who believe in His Son.

Then the question is: What is it that I am to believe about God's Son, Jesus Christ, which will lead God to give me eternal life with Him forever? And the beauty of God is that He never leaves us guessing, especially when it comes to having a personal relationship with Him, which He desires us to have. Therefore, we should not be surprised when God gives us the answer to our question in what He tells us at 1 Corinthians 15:1-4, "[1] Now I make known to you, brethren, the gospel which I preached to you, which also you received, in which also you stand, [2] by which also you are saved, if you hold fast the word which I preached to you, unless you believed in vain. [3] For I delivered to you as of first importance what I also received, that Christ died for our sins according to the Scriptures, [4] and that He was buried, and that He was raised on the third day according to the Scriptures..." Therefore, "the gospel," which simply means 'good news,' which God wants you to hear and believe in order to "be saved," which simply refers to you coming to know God and have eternal life with Him, is that His Son has already died for you, has already been buried, and has already been raised from the dead again the third day after His death, in order that God would have a basis by which to forgive you of all your sins, which are all against Him, and to freely give you eternal life with Him, for simply believing this message in your heart.

One thing which often prevents a person from believing the gospel at this point is not seeing oneself as a sinner before a Holy God. When we look at ourselves by our own assessment, and especially when we compare ourselves with others around us, we often think of ourselves as being better than others, and so good enough to enter Heaven in our present condition. The problem with this is that it is the product of our own thinking and is not God's assessment of our situation. God's assessment of our situation is as He tells us at Romans 3:10-12,23 in part, "[10] as it is written, "There is none righteous, not even one... [11] there is none who seeks for God [12] all have turned aside... there is none who does good, there is not even one... [23] for all have sinned and fall short of the glory of God..." Quite a different assessment of the human race from that which we as human beings often have of ourselves, is this not? But why would God have such an assessment of the whole human race? For the answer to that question, we need to be aware that God is Creator of all that exists, so that when God created the first man, Adam, at the beginning of time, God created him in innocence,

144

meaning that Adam as first created by God neither knew good nor evil, nor was there any sin anywhere in God's original sinless creation.

However, the day came when God tested Adam with a command, saying to him in the garden of Eden here on earth, which was the perfect environment which God had for him, what we now read at Genesis 2:16,17, "The Lord God commanded the man, saying, "From any tree of the garden you may eat freely; [17] but from the tree of the knowledge of good and evil you shall not eat, for in the day that you eat from it you will surely die." How important to see here that God gave Adam, who although a real person was also representative of the whole human race, the warning of the penalty of death for disobedience to His command.

Unfortunately, the day did come when Adam did partake of the forbidden tree and thereby did sin against God. The moment that happened, Adam not only became a sinner by practice, but also a sinner by nature. One thing my parents had to continually do while under their care was to restrain me from continually going the wrong way, for it seemed that of myself I could not do good, but kept going into sin. The reason this was happening is that from the age of accountability onwards, I had not only become a sinner by practice, but also a sinner by nature. And here the age of accountability needs to be seen as being when as a young child in innocence - which moment is known only by God - one comes to learn the right from the wrong and chooses the wrong, thereby becoming personally accountable to God for one's own sin against Him, since all sin is first of all against Him. And that is why God can say at Romans 3:23 above that "all have sinned and fall short of the glory of God," because God knows that all human beings will go the way of Adam, our representative man, which is also why God can say what He does in regards to the whole of the human race at Romans 5:12, where we read, "Therefore, just as through one man (Adam) sin entered into the world, and death through sin, and so death spread to all men, because all sinned" (from the age of accountability onward).

And so we see that the whole human race is declared by God to not only be sinners by practice and by nature from the age of accountability onwards, but the whole of the human race is now subject to death! In other words, in God's sight the whole of the human race is under the judgment of the penalty of death, due to all being sinners by practice and by nature. You will recall above, in the first verse we quoted from Romans 6:23, God did say there that "the wages of sin is death." And what God means by "death" here is not just loss of physical life, when the physical body we have dies, but also has spiritual death in mind, which is far worse! Spiritual death has its beginning when a separation takes place between a person and God at the moment one becomes a sinner at the age of accountability and ends after the final judgment of time, when God forever casts away from His Presence those who before physical death refused to believe in His Son, Jesus Christ, thereby personally forfeiting the forgiveness of their sins and eternal life with God. And now all such will pay the penalty for their own sins in hell, away from the Presence of God forever.

It is in the midst of such a hopeless situation in which the whole of the human race found itself in that God TOOK THE INITIATIVE and sent His own eternally existing Son into the world, as born of a virgin in the innocence of Adam – so as not to inherit the sinful nature passed on from generation after generation from Adam onwards – so that He might be the acceptable sacrifice offered to God His Father at the cross, there bearing our sins in His body, and there dying the death due our sins! God's Son, Jesus Christ, was then buried and raised from the dead the third day, to ever be alive, for it is through Him, on the basis of what God has done for us through His Son, that God The Father forgives our sins and imparts us eternal life.

Now, by God's grace and His enablement, may you see your need of God's Son to be Your Savior from the penalty due sin, which is death, not only physical, but also spiritual. And by God's grace, may He lead you to believe in His Son, Jesus Christ, and in believing, to receive the forgiveness of your sins and eternal life with Him forever! And based on the truth just shared, the author would now like to ask you a few questions, with the answer being just between yourself and God:

When God says at Romans 3:23, "for all have sinned and fall short of the glory of God," does that include you?

When God says at Romans 5:8, "But God demonstrates His own love toward us, in that while we were yet sinners, Christ died for us," were you included in Christ's death on behalf of sinners?

146

And when God further says at 1 Peter 3:18 in part, "For Christ also died for sins once for all, the just for the unjust, so that He might bring us to God, having been put to death in the flesh, but made alive in the spirit," were you part of the unjust for whom Christ died?

When God says at Romans 6:23, "For the wages of sin is death, but the free gift of God is eternal life in Christ Jesus our Lord," do you want that eternal life as a free gift from God?

When God says at John 3:16, "For God so loved the world, that He gave His only begotten Son, that whoever believes in Him shall not perish, but have eternal life," do you now believe that Jesus Christ is indeed God's Son in human flesh, Who came from Heaven to this earth to die in your place, so as to save you from ever experiencing the judgment of God leading to an eternal separation from God in hell?

And when God then further says to you at Isaiah 55:6, "Seek the Lord while He may be found; call upon Him while He is near," for His further promise to you here is as we read at Romans 10:9-11,13, "[9] that if you confess with your mouth Jesus as Lord, and believe in your heart that God raised Him from the dead, you will be saved (that is, you will now enter into a personal relationship with God by faith); [10] for with the heart a person believes, resulting in righteousness (that is, in now receiving God's own righteous life to live by), and with the mouth he confesses, resulting in salvation (that is, in now receiving as a free gift the forgiveness of sins and eternal life with God). [11] For the Scripture says, "Whoever believes in Him will not be disappointed..." [13] for "Whoever will call on the name of the Lord will be saved." Will you now call upon God from your heart, telling God in your own words your answer to each question that has just been asked?

The author's prayer for you at this point, as you now call upon God by His grace, is what we read at Romans 15:13, "Now may the God of hope fill you with all joy and peace in believing, so that you will abound in hope by the power of the Holy Spirit."

/ The next book

As this book is being published, God has given His servant the go-ahead to write a fifth book in "The Word Of God Library" series, titled, "God's Letter To Scattered Believers Through James." In case it is not, the reader may want to check with the author's website to see what other book has been published:

http://www.pilgrimpathwaypublications.com

And if you have enjoyed reading this book or any other of the author's books, please feel free to let family, friends, and co-workers know about this book and other books. The author is not on any social media sites, so he relies on God and readers like you to spread the word. May God bless you for doing so!

Made in the USA
Columbia, SC
05 October 2017